Peas, Beans and Lentils

THE ENGLISH KITCHEN

Peas, Beans and Lentils

GROWING AND COOKING

Gail Harland

equinox

SHEFFIELD UK BRISTOL CT

Published by Equinox Publishing Ltd.

UK: Office 415, The Workstation, 15 Paternoster Row, Sheffield, South Yorkshire S1 2BX

USA: ISD, 70 Enterprise Drive, Bristol, CT 06010

www.equinoxpub.com

First published 2026

British Library Cataloguing-in-Publication Data

A catalogue record for this book is available from the British Library.

ISBN-13 978 1 80050 877 4 (paperback)
978 1 80050 878 1 (ePDF)
978 1 80050 879 8 (ePub)

Library of Congress Cataloging-in-Publication Data

Names: Harland, Gail author
Title: Peas, beans and lentils : growing and cooking / Gail Harland.
Description: Bristol, CT : Equinox Publishing, 2026. | Series: The English kitchen | Includes bibliographical references and index. | Summary: "Peas, Beans and Lentils covers topics such as growing, cooking with and eating pulses and the wider historical and cultural aspects of legumes. This book includes recipes and will appeal to a wide range of people, from those who enjoy growing their own food, to families interested in vegetarian, vegan, and sustainable eating, for whom pulses are an important source of protein and other nutrients, and to anyone interested in the ethnocultural aspects of food"-- Provided by publisher.
Identifiers: LCCN 2026007606 (print) | LCCN 2026007607 (ebook) | ISBN 9781800508774 paperback | ISBN 9781800508781 pdf | ISBN 9781800508798 epub
Subjects: LCSH: Cooking (Natural foods) | Cooking (Peas) | Cooking (Beans) | Cooking (Lentils) | Cooking (Legumes) | Vegetable gardening | LCGFT: Cookbooks
Classification: LCC TX741 .H374 2026 (print) | LCC TX741 (ebook) | DDC 641.5/63--dc23/eng/20260325
LC record available at https://lccn.loc.gov/2026007606
LC ebook record available at https://lccn.loc.gov/2026007607

Typeset by Scribe Inc.

To all my hard-working colleagues at the
Norfolk and Norwich University Hospital,
and to Ash and Jonathan, with love

CONTENTS

FIG. 1. Jack and the Bean-stalk from *George Cruikshank's Fairy Library*, Part Two (1865).

INTRODUCTION

For those brought up on fairy tales and pantomimes, the story of Jack and the Beanstalk will likely be a part of their childhood. First published in 1734 as 'Jack Spriggins and the Enchanted Bean' in *Round About Our Coal Fire, Or Christmas Entertainments*, it was adapted by Benjamin Tabart as *The History of Jack and the Bean-Stalk* in 1807. The tale tells of the boy Jack and his widowed mother. Jack's mother was aghast to find that he had swapped the family cow for a handful of supposedly magic beans and in her anger, threw the beans out of the window. Gardeners will know how quickly beans can germinate and grow but Jack's beans were not the sort you can buy at your local garden centre and by the next morning, a beanstalk had already reached up to an enchanted world above the clouds. Today we may be aghast at Jack's subsequent behaviour; breaking and entering a giant's home, stealing his gold, abducting his talking harp, and finally the killing of an endangered species. We may however have more sympathy with that original exchange of a cow for some beans.

Although cows have played a crucial role in agriculture for societies around the world—providing milk, meat, soil-improving dung, and the power to pull ploughs and carts—in terms of economic efficiency, plant-based agricultural industries make a better use of resources than animal farming. The magic of beans, and other members of the legume family, including peas and lentils, is that these plants form associations with friendly soil bacteria which fix nitrogen from the air. This enables them to produce their own fertilizer and ensures that these leguminous seeds are higher in protein than other staple food crops such as rice, wheat and potatoes.

Plants are infinitely interesting and a look at the wonderful world of legumes demonstrates the amazing diversity of plant species. The bean family is a large and fascinating plant group that contains over 19,000 species. These include some of the world's most ornamental plants, including climbing wisteria; the attention-grabbing shrub, the pride of Barbados; and the fabulous jade vine, native to the Philippines. The intriguing *Baphia arenicola*, recently discovered in central Angola, is what is known as a geoxyle, living almost entirely underground. There are also a significant number of important food crops, many of which had been domesticated in prehistoric times. The word legume derives from the Latin *legūmen*. In the French-speaking world *légumes* just means vegetables and francophones refer to peas, beans and lentils as *les légumineuses*. In botanical terms, however, a legume or leguminous plant is a member of the plant family known as the *Leguminosae* or *Fabaceae*. The word legume actually refers to the seed-containing pods of these plants. As the pods dry, they split along a central suture, scattering the seed around the parent plant where they germinate and grow to develop into the next generation of plants.

Pulses are the seeds of legume plants that are grown to maturity and then harvested once they are dry. Common pulses include lentils, chickpeas, butter beans, red kidney beans and dried peas. Green beans such as French and runner beans, mangetout, and sugar snap peas in which the pods are eaten, and also fresh green peas, are usually considered vegetable crops rather than pulses. Though there is a lot of overlap in the use of these terms. Many varieties which are mainly used for dried pulses can also be eaten as green vegetables in the pods while young. Dal are dried, split pulses that do not require soaking before cooking.

The United Nations' Food and Agriculture Organization does not consider soya beans and peanuts to be pulses because they are grown primarily for the extraction of their edible oils. However, these beans

Fig. 2. Fruits and vegetables in a vintage French postcard.

obviously have numerous other important culinary uses. Tofu from soya has been consumed in China for over 2,000 years and it is hard to imagine the modern North American diet without peanut butter. Some legumes, notably clovers and alfalfa (also called lucerne), are used almost exclusively as forage crops for animals and are classified as cover crops. Sprouted alfalfa seeds, however, are often eaten in salads and sandwiches and the flowers of clover—made into a delightful, amber-coloured syrup—can be used as a honey substitute (see the recipe in the dessert section). Roger Phillips, in his book *Wild Food*, reports that red clover was eaten widely by indigenous North Americans and he includes recipes for clover salad and red clover wine.

People love stories, and telling stories has been one of the main ways humans have shared information throughout our history. The histories and myths that surround many plants can be endlessly fascinating. Peas, beans and lentils feature in many fairy tales, poetry and prose, from the 'Pease Porridge Hot' rhyme of John Newbery's *Mother Goose's Melody* to Hans Christian Andersen's *The Princess and the Pea* and Gwendolyn Brooks' poem 'The Bean Eaters,' first published in her 1960 collection of that name. Legumes also occur in the visual arts of many cultures, including the pottery of the Moche civilization of northern Peru (1–800 CE). Carved ivory edamame bean netsukes from the Japanese Edo period (1600–1868) reference the ritual exorcism associated with the lunar New Year there, during which soya beans are scattered to expel any demons from the household. In Northern Europe, pea pods have been associated with a number of Christian saints and with customs surrounding fertility and marriage. Exquisitely carved boxwood pea pods produced in the Netherlands from the late fifteenth to early sixteenth century were used as prayer beads. The Italian Baroque artist Giovanna Garzoni (1600–1670) includes several images of broad beans in her meticulous still life paintings. I include many tales of legumes from around the world and look at how the crops themselves, and their associated stories, have been spread alongside human migration and trade.

Modern concerns regarding sustainability and food miles, as well as financial worries in these credit-crunch times, have stimulated many people to experiment with growing their own food. Growing fruit or nuts can require quite an investment in terms of time, space, and the initial cost of the plants, but leguminous seeds are relatively inexpensive, so you do not have to trade in the family cow to purchase them. Many seeds can be started easily on the kitchen windowsill, and once planted outdoors, may begin to produce a crop within three months. This book will show you how to grow an interesting range of legumes. The variety and versatility of plants is fascinating to gardeners and there is always something new to learn about them. Even if you have been unsuccessful at growing vegetables in the past, it is worth exploring the extensive world of legumes to find something that will grow in your homes' conditions. You do not need to have a large garden; many will thrive in a large bucket of recycled compost. I have grown successful crops of runner beans in a window box, where they remained out of reach of the local rabbit population. And you certainly do not need to be an expert gardener.

As a paediatric allergy dietitian working for the National Health Service, I am obviously concerned with the health implications of diet. Peas, beans and lentils all have excellent protein content with amino acid profiles that complement grains, such as wheat and rice. Legumes are useful sources of dietary fibre and many vitamins as well as minerals such as iron and calcium, while also being low in fat. They are of particular importance for those following vegetarian and vegan diets. Studies have shown that regular inclusion of peas and beans within a balanced diet may have protective heart and colon effects for everyone. Pea, soya bean and other pulse proteins are increasingly being used in dairy free milk alternatives, gluten free products, and sports drinks.

The bean family is vast and, as with any family, there may be members you do not get along with. The high fibre content of pulses can cause digestive problems including wind and bloating. Some legumes contain toxins and may require thorough preparation to make them safe to eat. Favism (glucose-6-phosphate dehydrogenase deficiency) is the most common enzyme deficiency anaemia worldwide and may result in haemolytic anaemia if affected people eat fava beans. Some people are allergic to legumes, most commonly peanut, soya bean and lupin. Legume allergies seem to be more common in people from the Mediterranean region. Fortunately, most sufferers are only allergic to one or a few legumes and can eat the others without problems.

Included in this book are more than 60 recipes which have their origins all around the world. The recipes I have chosen are generally very simple to cook. I enjoy the meditative slow stirring of a pot on the hob but I am easily distracted by whatever is outside the kitchen window and do not want to faff around with complicated culinary procedures. You will neither find long lists of difficult to obtain ingredients nor expensive, essential equipment. Mine is a low-tech kitchen. I do not possess a pressure cooker, a food processor, or an air fryer. A simple hand blender is useful for soups, purees, and baby foods but the beauty of beans is that you can cook your own delicious and nutritious meals with nothing more complicated than a saucepan and a wooden spoon.

Chapter 1
MEET THE FAMILY

Draw yourself up from the light of the moon,
And let them pass, as they will too soon,
With the bean-flowers' boon,
And the blackbird's tune,
And May, and June!

Robert Browning, *De Gustibus* (1855)

Peas, beans and lentils are members of the botanical family alternatively called *Fabaceae* or *Leguminosae*. It is a large and varied family with members ranging from small, low growing herbaceous plants such as kidney vetch (*Anthyllis vulneraria*), that is the sole food plant for the larvae of the small blue butterfly, to the massive Brazilian tree species *Dinizia jueirana-facao*, that was first described scientifically as recently as 2017 and is possibly the world's heaviest living organism. The scientific classification and naming of plants, known as taxonomy, can seem to be complicated and gardeners frequently complain that taxonomists are forever changing their minds and renaming plants. The common garden pea for example, was given the scientific name *Pisum sativum* (meaning 'cultivated pea') by Carl Linnaeus in 1753. Recent genetic studies however place the pea in the genus *Lathyrus* and it is now listed on Plants of the

World Online, the database of the Royal Botanic Gardens, Kew, as the species *Lathyrus oleraceus*. Not all botanists however agree with this change and the old name is still widely used. The rice bean was previously classified as *Phaseolus calcaratus var. gracilis* but after more study it has now been transferred to the genus *Vigna* as *Vigna gracilicaulis*.

Nomenclature

According to the International Association for Plant Taxonomy there are an estimated 350,500 species of plants on the planet, with many more yet to be discovered. Indeed some 2,000 new plant species are described and published each year by the global botanical community. The system of naming plant species is based on the work of the Swedish botanist, physician and zoologist Carl Linnaeus (1707–1778). He published the first edition of his *Systema Naturae* in 1735, at the age of 28, while studying in the Netherlands. This work established what is now known as the binomial nomenclature of plants, whereby each species can be identified by two names. The first part of the name identifies the genus to which a plant belongs, while the second name identifies the particular species within that genus. Hence all chickpeas are identified by the generic name *Cicer*. Cicer is the Latin word for chickpea and is thought to be the origin of the surname Cicero, made famous by the Roman statesman and philosopher Marcus Tullius Cicero (106–43 BCE). The cultivated chickpea used to make hummus is distinguished from its relatives by the specific name *arietinum* which means 'small ram,' based on the somewhat fanciful idea that the shape of the seed resembles the head of a ram.

Scientific plant names are always written in the Latin alphabet. This is because plant taxonomy, as we know it today, has its origins in Europe and Latin was used as the common language among European people. The first letter of the genus name should be written as a capital letter but that of the species name is in the lower case. Both parts of the name are italicized in normal text. Technically, a name is only complete if it is accompanied by an authority, demonstrating

Fig. 3. Chickpeas.

who gave the plant its name. Authority names are usually abbreviated, so for example Linnaeus becomes L. The chickpea therefore should be written as *Cicer arietinum* L. Use of this name, in theory at least, reduces the confusion that can arise through the multiple common names the plant may have, including not just chickpea but also garbanzo bean, gram, Bengal gram, Egyptian pea, chole and channa.

The rules of plant naming are set out in the International Code of Nomenclature for algae, fungi, and plants (ICN), the primary purpose of which is to avoid confusion by ensuring a plant has only one correct name. The first code of nomenclature was compiled by the French-Swiss botanist Alphonse de Candolle (1806–1893) who published his *Lois de la Nomenclature Botanique* in 1867. The international system of naming organisms was the first global scientific standard, predating standard calendars and units of measurement. The Code is amended every six years at an International Botanical Congress (IBC) to allow for changes in scientific thought. Botanists want plant classification to reflect our best understanding of evolutionary relationships and the subject has been revolutionised by developments in the study of plant DNA. These have revealed that some previous ideas about plant relationships were incorrect, so that names may need to change to reflect current research.

A species, as defined in the Royal Horticultural Society *Shorter Dictionary of Gardening*, consists of a group of 'closely related, morphologically similar individuals, often found within a distinct geographical range.' A group of closely related species is known as a genus (plural genera). Genera that have similar characteristics and are evolutionarily related are grouped into plant families. There are nearly 800 accepted genera in the *Fabaceae* which is the third largest plant family worldwide after the daisy family (*Asteraceae*) and the orchid family (*Orchidaceae*). The family name is usually formed from the most characteristic genus (the so-called type genus) within that family, so the name *Fabaceae* comes from genus *Faba*. Unfortunately, due to further research, *Faba* is now an obsolete genus, as it has been included within the genus *Vicia*. In Latin 'faba' means bean and *Vicia faba* is the scientific name for fava/faba beans, also known as broad beans.

Plant family names usually end in the suffix -aceae. The use of the older family name *Leguminosae* is an accepted alternative name for *Fabaceae*, because the 1978 International Code of Botanical Nomenclature (ICBN) permits the use of alternative names for eight families that are 'sanctioned by long usage.' The *Fabaceae* family is divided into three subfamilies, the *Faboideae* (pea subfamily), the *Caesalpinioideae* (palo-verde subfamily), and the *Mimosoideae* (the mesquite subfamily). Each subfamily has distinctive flower structures that make them readily recognizable. There has been much debate within the botanical community as to whether these subfamilies warrant recognition as separate families in their own right. Molecular studies indicate that the legumes are best treated as one large family.

All newly-described species will have a type specimen, which is the original specimen on which the description is based. For plants, these are usually found in the herbarium collections of major botanical gardens. The type specimen for *Cicer arietinum* is held at the herbarium of the Royal Botanic Gardens, Kew. The type specimen for the human species *Homo sapiens* is the remains of Linnaeus himself, which are buried in Uppsala Cathedral in Sweden, as he himself was the only specimen he is known to have examined when writing the original species description.

Species vary considerably in the wild but distinctions may be made, usually on the basis of geographical distinctiveness. Particular naturally-occurring differences from the standard species can be distinguished. The horse bean or field bean, for example, a small-seeded variety of the broad bean plant commonly grown for animal feed is sometimes referred to as *Vicia faba* var. *equina* although botanically that is considered the same as Vicia faba.

A cultivar is a particular variety of a plant in cultivation that can be reproduced either vegetatively or by seed to produce more of the same plant. It can have arisen either as a selected natural plant or through deliberate hybridisation. The name of the cultivar follows the genus and species name. It is written in the language of the person who described it, in single quotation marks and should not be translated. For example, a chickpea cultivar raised at the Indian Institute of Science Education and Research at Berhampur in eastern India and known for its resistance to Fusarium wilt was released in 2004 as *Cicer arietinum* 'Anuradha.'

The common names of peas and beans may seem simpler to use than scientific nomenclature. However, there can be confusion even as to what is a pea and what a bean. There is actually no strict definition as to which is which and as we have seen, some such as *Cicer arietinum* can be called by either name. It is usually known as the *chickpea* in the United Kingdom and Australia but more often by the Spanish-derived name *garbanzo bean* in the United States and Canada. (Chickpeas are known as *pois chiche* in French). The specific name *Cajanus cajan* refers to the pulse commonly known as the pigeon pea, but an alternative name for this is Congo bean. Peas are generally thought to be of a more spherical shape in comparison to beans. Bean shapes vary widely but often have a kidney-shaped appearance. The scientific name for lentils, *Lens culinaris* (now *Vicia lens*), comes from the curved, lens-shaped seeds. There is a wide range of colours of peas, beans and lentils, and beans in particular can have wonderful distinctive markings and speckles.

Evolution of Legumes

There is an abundant and diverse fossil record of plants in the bean family, especially for the period following the Cretaceous–Paleogene extinction event around 66 million years ago, when three-quarters of the plant and animal species on Earth became extinct.

The earliest fossils found that can be definitively assigned to the *Fabaceae* were thought to have appeared in the early Palaeocene (approximately 65 million years ago). However, in 2021 Naylet Centeno-González of the National Autonomous University of Mexico reported the discovery in the Olmos Formation of Mexico of a legume fruit fossil estimated at 73.5 million years old. Designated as *Leguminocarpum olmensis*, this fossil significantly extends the record into the Cretaceous period. More than 500 fossil specimens—including flowers, fruit, leaves, wood, and pollen—collected from coal and clay open-pit mines in Colombia and dated to about 58–60 million years old, show distinctive legume features and indicate that they were abundant in the earliest rainforests in northern South America. In the Eocene, from approximately 33.9–56 million years ago, the family was already diverse in many fossil assemblages around the world.

It is thought that legumes probably first appeared during the Cretaceous period in Africa and migrated to South America and subsequently North America, before reaching Eurasia. The subfamilies *Caesalpinioideae*, *Mimosoideae*, and *Faboideae* were already in existence by the Cretaceous. Fossil leaves and fruits referable to the *Faboideae* from the late Palaeocene have been found in northwestern Wyoming in the United States. Legume fruits and leaves assigned to the genus *Wisteria* have been dated to the Miocene period (5.33–23.03 million years ago) in China.

The advent of molecular techniques has allowed significant advances in the study of the evolutionary development and diversification of species. DNA barcoding, that involves the use of specific gene regions to identify species, has been utilized to examine various legume species. Results indicate that these three subfamilies originated nearly simultaneously, challenging the traditional view of some subfamilies as 'basal' or 'early-diverging.' It seems instead that the family rapidly adapted to various geographical regions, leading to its current widespread distribution. Findings on the evolution of nitrogen-fixing nodules also have biogeographical implications, as the ability to fix nitrogen would have allowed *Fabaceae* species to colonize nutrient-poor soils across different continents.

Large fossil beans, *Jantungspermum gunnellii*, that are among the largest seeds in the fossil record, were discovered in Indonesian Borneo and have been dated to the Eocene period, approximately 34–40 million years ago. These are thought to provide the first macrofossil evidence of a plant lineage moving from Asia into Australia after the Asia-Australia tectonic collision. These fossil seeds represent a now-extinct legume genus that grew in Southeast Asia and was related to the existing *Castanospermum australe*. Known as the black bean or Moreton Bay chestnut, this tree is found today only in the coastal rainforests of northern Australia and neighbouring islands.

Characteristics of the Bean Family

Members of the *Fabaceae* are found everywhere on Earth except in Antarctica and the High Arctic. The trees often grow in tropical regions, while shrubs and herbaceous plants are predominant in more temperate climates. Common characteristics include:

- Plant forms encompass trees, shrubs, climbers, herbaceous perennials, and annuals.
- The leaves are arranged alternately up the stem and are most often compound (divided into three or more leaflets). However, leaves of a few species, such as the Judas tree (*Cercis siliquastrum*), are simple or reduced to scales. The margins of the leaflets are usually smooth.
- Plants frequently form visible nodules on the roots due to an established symbiotic relationship with nitrogen-fixing bacteria.
- The flowers have five fused sepals and five petals. They are bisexual (having both stamens and a pistil) with radial or bilateral symmetry.
- The fruit is a legume or pod that usually releases seeds by splitting open along two seams, although some, such as peanuts (*Arachis hypogaea*) and carobs (*Ceratonia siliqua*), do not naturally open.

Differences between the subfamilies:

- Subfamily *Mimosoideae* have flowers with small, often inconspicuous petals but numerous showy, prominent stamens. Members, including *Acacia* and *Mimosa*, are mostly shrubs and trees and grow predominantly in tropical and subtropical regions. Some may be armed with spines as a defence against herbivores and in some *Vachellia* species swollen thorn bases have evolved as homes for resident ants.
- Subfamily *Caesalpinioideae* are mainly trees growing in the moist tropics, for example the well-named flamboyant tree, *Delonix regia*, native to Madagascar. This group often has bipinnate leaves (twice divided into smaller leaflets) and flowers with bilateral symmetry.
- Subfamily *Faboideae* is by far the largest and most diverse of the three subfamilies. Its members typically have bilaterally symmetrical flowers like those of the pea, with two wing petals, two lower petals fused together to form a keel, and a large standard petal held behind the wing petals. This flower shape is thought to resemble butterflies (hence the other name of the group, *Papilionoideae* which arises from *papilio*, meaning butterfly). There are 10 stamens of which nine are fused together.

Legumes are well known for their ability to fix nitrogen which usually occurs in special nodules that form on the roots, although not all genera form nodules. Most members of the subfamilies *Faboideae* and *Mimosoideae* seem to be capable of nodulating, but very few members of *Caesalpinioideae* do so. The German agricultural chemist Hermann Hellriegel (1831–1895) showed that leguminous plants took nitrogen from the atmosphere and released it in the soil and discovered that this occurred in the nodules on the plant roots. The first person to describe the symbiotic interaction between legumes and nitrogen-fixing root bacteria was the Dutch microbiologist Martinus Willem Beijerinck (1851–1931), who was an expert on plant galls. He isolated a bacterium from the root nodules of *Vicia* in 1888 which he named *Bacillus radicicola*. This is now classified as *Rhizobium* and many other species have since been described which are given the general name rhizobia.

Rhizobia infect the roots of the host plant, and as they multiply, they generate a response from the plant leading to the localized growth of the periderm tissues of the root's outer layer. This develops into the root nodule. The bacteria live there supplied with the sugars

FIG. 4. The garden pea, showing parts of a typical pea family member.

made by the plant through the process of photosynthesis. They convert atmospheric nitrogen into ammonia and then transform this into nitrogen compounds that can be absorbed by the plant. Rhizobia can also infect roots of non-nodulating legumes and such plants have demonstrated the ability to also fix nitrogen.

Nitrogen compounds are essential for the basic building blocks of all living beings, being part of the nucleotides for DNA and RNA, and the amino acids that make proteins. Although nitrogen is abundant in nature, forming 78% of the Earth's atmosphere, it is a relatively inert gas and converting nitrogen gas to usable compounds like ammonia or nitrate is difficult, so the ability to fix nitrogen gives legumes a competitive edge in areas with limited available nitrogen in the soil. When the plants die the nitrogen becomes available for other crops. Prior to the development of industrial synthesis of urea from atmospheric nitrogen by the German chemists Fritz Haber and Carl Bosch in the early 20th century, that is the basis for modern synthetic agricultural fertilizers, planting legumes in agricultural fields was the most common and sustainable way to replenish the nitrogen in the soil. Planting legumes in rotation with other crops is known as crop rotation and has been practised for thousands of years to encourage the sustained fertility of the soil.

More than 2,300 years ago, Androsthenes of Thasos, one of the trierarchs of the Hydaspes Fleet of Alexander the Great in 324 BCE, explored Bahrain and the Arabian coast. He wrote vivid descriptions of the flora he encountered there and was intrigued by the way some legumes appear to sleep at night by folding up their leaves. This process, known as nyctinasty (night movement), involves the circadian, rhythmic folding of plant leaves or leaflets at night and their opening at daytime. Nastic responses are usually fast, reversible movements rather than growth responses. Charles Darwin recruited his son Francis to assist in lengthy studies documenting the range of movements in plants, during which he reported to Sir Joseph Hooker, 'we have killed or badly injured a multitude of plants.' His results, reported in *The Power of Movement in Plants* (1880), found that the legume family includes many more nyctinastic species than all other families combined. Fossil evidence of ancient insect-nibbled leaves has indicated that plants were doing this 250 million years ago.

Studies of the monkey pod or rain tree (*Samanea saman*), a large tree native to Central and South America, have shown that nyctinasty in leguminous plants is caused by changes in the volume of cells in a special organ known as the pulvinus, located at the base of the leaflet. Swelling and shrinking of the motor cells is considered analogous to that of guard cells in the stoma of leaves that allow gaseous exchange. The genes involved in the development of pulvini have been identified using a 'sleepless' mutation of *Lotus japonicus* which showed defects in leaf movements. In this plant the pulvinus had been replaced with a petiole-like structure.

Like nitrogen fixing roots, nyctinastic leaf movements are thought to be another competitive advantage of legumes in less-than-ideal environments. In studies comparing beans (*Phaseolus vulgaris*) and peanut with maize, okra, safflower and sesame, researchers have discovered that while all six crops grow taller with less branching and fewer flowers when overcrowded, the total harvest of the legumes remains unaffected while that of the other four species is significantly reduced. Researchers speculate that the legumes can tolerate higher population densities because leaf movement in the evening allows them to catch the last light of the day, causing them to develop more like unshaded plants. Plants in the genera *Neptunia* and *Mimosa* can also show special leaf movements known as seismonasty which are prompted by touch. This may be a response to evade herbivores. The sensitive plant (*Mimosa pudica*) is the best-known species to exhibit this and is often grown as a 'pet' house plant. Perhaps more dramatic is the Asian shrub *Codariocalyx motorius*, the telegraph or dancing plant, which Darwin called a 'vegetable wonder.' The small leaflets at the base of its compound leaves move around as if they were semaphoring. The Indian polymath Jagadish Chandra Bose used the plant in his experiments into plant perception. The nastic movements increase in speed with increasingly bright light or higher temperatures but scientists are still uncertain what purpose they serve.

Many legumes are climbing plants. The climbing habit is thought to have developed several times in distinct plant lineages throughout their evolutionary history. It is likely a response to competition for light. Plants can use many different mechanisms to climb. Runner beans and wisteria have twining stems. Some species, such as *Wisteria floribunda*, twine in a clockwise direction, while others, including the Chinese species *Wisteria sinensis*, twine in an anti-clockwise direction. Many legumes climb by means of tendrils which are thread-like structures developed from specialized stems or leaves. In the garden pea, it is only the terminal leaflets that are modified to become tendrils whereas in yellow vetch (*Lathyrus aphaca*), the whole leaf becomes a tendril.

Flowers are not specifically designed for our enjoyment but have always been admired and valued by humans. Around 12,000 years ago in the Carmel Mountain range of what is now northern Israel, the Natufian people lined graves of their loved ones with soft mud which they covered with a layer of fresh flowering plants to provide a colourful and fragrant resting place for the deceased. In the legume family, the sweet pea, *Lathyrus odoratus*, native to Sicily, southern Italy and the Aegean Islands, has been a treasured garden plant for hundreds of years and decorates the pages of many illuminated manuscripts of the medieval period. As the name suggests, it is greatly prized for its sweet fragrance. Cultivars such as 'Cupani' and 'Cedric Morris' are very close to the wild species and superbly scented, although many twentieth-century cultivars are grown more for their flamboyant looks than their fragrance.

Sweet peas, like most other members of the subfamily *Faboideae*, are entomophilous plants, which means they are pollinated by insects. The flowers are typically showy to attract pollinators. The evolution of flowers with a keel within the bean family and others, including *Polygalaceae*, is thought to have been driven by bees. Keeping the pollen hidden within the keel gives it some protection from the elements but also reduces the chance of the pollinator making off with pollen and nectar without having performed the service of pollination. Studies in Algeria looking at pollination of the broad bean found that the wild bee *Eucera pulveracea* was the most abundant visitor and seemed to be the most effective pollinator. However, many visits by honey bees (*Apis mellifera*) and all visits by violet carpenter bees (*Xylocopa violacea*) involved 'nectar robbery,' by which the nectar was taken through holes made by the bees at the base of the flower. Interestingly even flowers visited by 'robber bees' show improved pod set relative to no visitation.

Less commonly, legumes may be butterfly-pollinated, as in the West African tree *Berlinia grandiflora*; fly-pollinated, for example, by the potato bean *Apios americana*; or pollinated by beetles, as in the Australian shrub *Aotus lanigera*. Some species with large and brightly-coloured flowers may be bird-pollinated. The coral tree

Erythrina speciosa, for example, is pollinated by hummingbirds. More than ten mammal species including squirrels, flying foxes, and macaques have been recorded as pollinators of *Mucuna macrocarpa*, an evergreen, climbing vine that is widely distributed in the subtropical and temperate islands of Southeast Asia. The plant provides its furry visitors with ample supplies of nectar that has a high sucrose content in return for their pollination services. The Central American vine *Mucuna holtonii* is usually pollinated by the Commissaris's long-tongued bat (*Glossophaga commissarisi*) and even provides special acoustic guide petals which act like tiny satellite dishes to bounce the bats' sonar signals back towards them.

As Robert Browning noted, bean-flowers can be a boon and they often have a pleasing perfume (see quote at the beginning of this chapter). The British gardener and horticultural writer Eleanour Sinclair Rohde (1881–1950) observed in her book *The Scented Garden* (1931), 'Few people appreciate the scent of broad bean flowers, simply because the broad bean is a "vegetable," yet it is one of the most beautiful of flower scents.' The wonderful coconut scent of the common gorse (*Ulex europaeus*) makes any walk through heathland a pleasure. Flowers' scents, of course, are not designed for human delight but to attract pollinators and enable the setting of seeds. Floral scents are mixtures of volatile organic compounds with a prevalence of monoterpenes. Pollinators and plants evolved together so that red flowers pollinated by birds tend not to be fragrant because birds rely more on vision than scent, for example the parrot bill *Clianthus puniceus.* Bat-pollinated plants such as the bitter bean (*Parkia speciosa*) of Southeast Asia, attract their pollinators by emitting floral scents rich in sulphur-containing compounds. In wind-pollinated flowers, scent may act to ward off pests. Wind pollination is not common in legumes but is found in the tree *Ateleia herbert-smithii.*

Plant emissions of volatile organic compounds are affected by climatic variables such as temperature and humidity and by other environmental factors including light, carbon dioxide concentration, and wind speed. Composition of scent emission can vary relative to the time of day. Moth pollinated plants, such as the Brazilian leguminous orchid tree (*Bauhinia forficata*), typically have white petals and

Fig. 5. Broad bean flower with a bumblebee visitor.

emit strong floral scents after dusk but have no noticeable fragrance during the day. Air pollution can reduce the abilities of pollinating insects to detect flower scent. Nitrogenous oxides and ozone alter the structure of odour molecules, making it difficult for insects to pick them up.

The most characteristic part of a legume plant is the seed pod which typically splits along two seams. The pod provides protection for the developing seeds and also helps to supply sugars by photosynthesis while it remains green. *Fabaceae* seeds are typically kidney shaped or spherical. The hilum, a scar where the seed was attached to the pod, is a prominent feature, and a ridge called the raphe may also be visible. Seeds often exhibit physical dormancy due to a hard seed coat that restricts water uptake, influencing germination.

The largest legume pods, which can reach up to two metres (6.5′) in length, are those of the sea bean or monkey ladder (*Entada gigas*). Native to the rainforests of tropical America and Africa, its very wide geographical distribution has been enabled by the ability of its huge pods to travel great distances down rivers and across seas to start new colonies. There are many other species known as sea beans or drift seeds that are adapted for long-distance dispersal by water. They can drift for thousands of kilometres through ocean currents and, like the coconut, be found on distant shores. Drift seeds provide valuable information for scientists who study ocean currents. The

Fig. 6. Seed pods of *Vachellia nilotica* (*Acacia nilotica*).

International Sea-bean Symposium has been held annually since 1996 for scientists, botanists, oceanographers, and beachcombers dedicated to the study of drift seeds.

Legume fruits are very variable and use several different methods to disperse their seeds. Some species of *Tipuana* trees have helicopter-like seeds which are adapted for wind dispersal. The most common dispersal method is an explosive technique known as ballochory, employed by gorse, lupins, and the garden pea. These rely on the warmth of the sun to dry the seed pods. The side of the pod facing the sun dries out more quickly than the side in the shade, causing the pod to buckle and split along the sutures. The seed pods then rapidly curl up, expelling the seeds some distance from the parent plant. If you stand quietly by a gorse bush on a hot, dry day in late summer, you can actually hear the seed pods popping. Leguminous orchid trees (*Bauhinia* spp.) bear large pods that can fling seeds nearly fifteen metres (49′) away. Seed-eating rodents such as field mice and squirrels may be considered pests but can actually assist plants with long-range seed dispersal. Although they will eat a proportion of the seed immediately, they often store seeds in caches for times of scarcity. Any seed that they fail to return for will have the opportunity to germinate and to grow away from competition with the parent plant.

Family Members

Legumes for Ornamental and Other Purposes

Although members of the bean family have of course been valued for food for thousands of years, there are many plants within the family that have been treasured for other purposes. For example, the valuable timber of the rosewoods or the ancient indigo dye which comes from the shrub *Indigofera tinctoria*. Brazilwood (*Paubrasilia echinata*), which gave the country Brazil its name, is the preferred wood for violin bows, and a source of red dye. Its populations have been threatened by over-harvesting and habitat destruction. Legumes are used as pharmaceuticals, insecticides, soaps, textiles, gums, resins and bio-fuels. Archaeological evidence shows that beans of

Anadenanthera peregrina, the jopo, have been used in northern South America and the Caribbean as hallucinogens for thousands of years.

Some legumes are grown simply because they are jaw-droppingly beautiful. There are just two species of laburnum, sometimes called the golden chain or golden rain tree, *Laburnum anagyroides*, the common laburnum and *L. alpinum*, the alpine laburnum. They are native to the mountains of southern Europe from France to the Balkans. The famous laburnum arch at Bodnant Gardens near Conwy in Wales, planted by Henry Pochin in 1880, has inspired many similar creations. This 55-metre-long tunnel of golden flowers is a spectacular sight at its peak flowering from the end of May to the beginning of June. All parts of the laburnum are poisonous so should not be eaten, although fatalities are very rare. As a child, I once experimented with stepping on the head of a garden rake to see if it would spring up and hit you, as seen in assorted Looney Toons cartoons (it does, and it hurts), but even with my predilection for personal research, I was sufficiently aware that you should not experiment with laburnum seeds.

Wisteria, one of the most loved of all climbing plants, is a vigorous vine with long racemes of flowers in shades of lilac, purple, pink or white. There are four species native to China, Japan, Korea, Vietnam, and the eastern United States. Many different cultivars have been raised and many are beautifully fragrant. The Kawachi Fujien Wisteria Garden in the hills to the southwest of Kitakyushu, in Fukuoka Prefecture, Japan has two spectacular 100-metre-long tunnels of blue and white wisteria that attract admirers from all around the world but the world's largest wisteria is thought to be the Sierra Madre wisteria in California which covers an area of more than 1 acre (0.40 ha). The flower petals of wisteria can be eaten. I find they taste somewhat soapy on their own but they look pretty and are lovely when scattered through a mixed salad. The seeds of all wisteria species however contain high levels of toxic lectins and the glycoside wisterin. As little as half a seed can cause severe gastrointestinal symptoms in young children.

Strongylodon macrobotrys, commonly known as the jade vine, is native to the rainforests of the Philippines. It has wisteria-like racemes of flowers in a mesmerizing jade-green colour. It needs a minimum temperature of 15°C (59°F) to grow and is cultivated in glasshouses around the world. The jade vine is pollinated by bats in the wild, so cultivated plants have to be hand-pollinated in order to bear fruit. These will mature to be the size of a melon. Like those of wisteria, jade vine flowers are edible and are eaten as vegetables on the island of Luzon, the largest island in the Philippines. The red jade vine or New Guinea creeper (*Mucuna bennettii*) is another spectacular exotic for tropical climates or under glass.

Native to the North Island of New Zealand, *Clianthus puniceus* has striking clusters of red flowers that have inspired the common names of lobster claw and parrot bill. It likely evolved for pollination by birds such as the tūī (*Prosthemadera novaeseelandiae*). These plants are not fully frost-hardy but are worth trialling in a sheltered position and always attract attention when in flower. Another New Zealand native is *Sophora microphylla*, the small-leaved kowhai, which is an evergreen shrub or small tree that is thought to have been used by giant moa birds for nesting material and food. Gardeners plant it for its attractive foliage and profusion of golden bells in the springtime. The inedible pods of the related *Sophora tomentosa* have been used in Africa to make fish poisons and insect repellents.

Ambatch (*Aeschynomene elaphroxylon*), also known as the Nile pith-tree, is a large shrub or small tree that grows in the swamps, lakes and rivers of tropical Africa. It has an extremely lightweight, spongy wood which acts as a float and a highly-adapted root system that forms a tangled web hanging in the water enabling it to grow as a floating island. Its timber, one of the lightest of known woods, is rot-resistant and is traditionally used to make floats for fishing nets as well as canoes and rafts.

Food Plants of the Fabaceae

The UN's Food and Agriculture Organization (FAO) recognizes eleven groups of staple pulses.

1. Dry beans (in the genera *Phaseolus* and *Vigna*)
    - Kidney bean, navy bean, pinto bean, black turtle bean, haricot bean (*Phaseolus vulgaris*)
    - Lima bean, butter bean (*Phaseolus lunatus*)
    - Adzuki bean, azuki bean (*Vigna angularis*)
    - Mung bean, golden gram, green gram (*Vigna radiata*)
    - Black gram, urad (*Vigna mungo*)
    - Scarlet runner bean (*Phaseolus coccineus*)
    - Rice bean (*Vigna gracilicaulis*)
    - Moth bean (*Vigna aconitifolia*)
    - Tepary bean (*Phaseolus acutifolius*)
2. Dry broad beans (*Vicia faba*)
    - Horse bean (*Vicia faba equina*)
    - Broad bean (*Vicia faba*)
    - Field bean (*Vicia faba*)
3. Dry peas (*Pisum* spp.)
    - Garden pea (*Pisum sativum* var. *sativum*)
    - Protein pea (*Pisum sativum* var. *arvense*)
4. Chickpea, garbanzo, Bengal gram (*Cicer arietinum*)
5. Dry cowpea, black-eyed pea, blackeye bean (*Vigna unguiculata*)
6. Pigeon pea, Arhar/Toor, cajan pea, Congo bean, gandules (*Cajanus cajan*)
7. Lentil (*Vicia lens*, formerly *Lens culinaris*)
8. Bambara groundnut, earth pea (*Vigna subterranea*)
9. Vetch, common vetch (*Vicia sativa*)
10. Lupins (*Lupinus* spp.)
11. Minor pulses, including:
    - Lablab, hyacinth bean (*Lablab purpureus*)
    - Jack bean (*Canavalia ensiformis*), sword bean (*Canavalia gladiata*)
    - Winged bean (*Psophocarpus tetragonolobus*)
    - Velvet bean, cowitch (*Mucuna pruriens var. utilis*)
    - Yam bean (*Pachyrhizus erosus*)

Beans

The common bean (*Phaseolus vulgaris*) was first described scientifically in 1753, but may have been domesticated as much as 8,000 years earlier, first in Mexico, then with separate lineages in Mesoamerica and in the southern Andes region. Both the pods and the beans themselves are highly variable in appearance. Members of this species include the kidney bean, navy bean, pinto bean, black turtle bean, haricot bean/vert, black bean, borlotti bean, rashti bean, flageolet, green bean and white bean. There are many other variations that have arisen through cultivation grown throughout the world. It is a scrambling annual plant with long twining stems and grows primarily in seasonally dry habitats. Wild plants are climbers, but selections in cultivation are classified either as bush beans or climbing/pole beans depending on their style of growth. Very young leaves are sometimes eaten as a salad green while the older leaves can be cooked. A toxic lectin called phytohaemagglutinin is present in many common bean varieties but is especially concentrated in red kidney beans which have three times the quantity that white kidney beans do. Green, French, or string beans are the young, unripe fruits of various cultivars of the common bean, eaten as green vegetables.

The lima bean or butter bean (*Phaseolus lunatus*), sometimes known as the double bean or Madagascar bean, originated in the Americas from Mexico to Peru. It is a scrambling annual or perennial and produces beans that are usually larger than the common bean. They have a mealy texture. There is a small-seeded variety known as the Sieva type found distributed from Mexico to Argentina. Lima beans were very important to the Moche culture of northern Peru. In Valencia, Spain they are called garrofón and are an important constituent of paella. Bush and climbing forms are available and there are different cultivars with beautifully speckled beans. As with common beans, lima beans must be boiled for at least ten minutes to deactivate the phytohaemagglutinin content.

The adzuki or azuki bean (*Vigna angularis*), also called the red mung bean, is an Asian species, native from Nepal to South China and in northern Indo-China, Taiwan, and Japan. It is a scrambling annual or perennial and grows in temperate conditions. The plants are not frost-hardy and needs soil temperatures above 6–10°C (43–50°F) to germinate. The pods are 8–12 cm (3–5″) long and contain between five and ten seeds. The beans are quite small (approximately 5 mm long). The most common cultivars have chestnut-red beans but there are also white, black, grey, and mottled varieties. In Japan, the adzuki bean is the second most important legume after the soya bean. It is commonly used in sweet as well as savoury dishes.

The mung bean (*Vigna radiata*) grows wild on the Arabian Peninsula, Taiwan to tropical Asia, and northern and eastern Australia. It is an annual climbing plant with yellow, self-pollinating flowers. It requires a hot climate for germination and growth. Each plant usually produced 30–50 long thin pods which have a fuzzy down. Like adzuki beans, the small green beans are eaten in sweet and savoury foods. In Europe and North America, they are mainly used as bean sprouts. The sprouts can be stir-fried as a vegetable accompaniment to a Chinese meal, used in spring rolls, and are a major ingredient in much Malaysian cuisine.

Believed to have been first domesticated in India around 4,500 years ago, black gram, urad, or the urd bean (*Vigna mungo*) is very widely used in Indian cuisine. It grows best in areas of low humidity where annual daytime temperatures are within the range 22–35°C (72–95°F). Too much rain at flowering time reduces seed yield. Wild plants are annual climbers with large hairy leaves and yellow flowers, but the most widely grown domesticated crop is a bushy plant growing up to one metre tall. A breeding programme started in India in 1967 resulted in the release of more than 85 cultivars, mostly selected for disease and pest resistance. While the skin of the black gram bean is black, the interior is white. When split, the beans are sometimes sold as white lentils.

Originating in Central America, the scarlet runner bean (*Phaseolus coccineus*), was introduced to Europe in the mid-seventeenth century where it was originally grown as an ornamental plant. These are perennial vines which form tuberous roots, but are usually treated as annuals in colder climates. The starchy roots are eaten in Mesoamerica. Most varieties have red flowers and multi-coloured seeds although some have white flowers and white seeds. A selection with particularly large white beans is used to make gigantes plaki, a Greek dish composed of beans stewed in a tomato sauce. Wild runner beans are naturally short-day plants that do not flower until the nights are more than ten hours long. In the United Kingdom this does not occur until September, so the plants would only have a month or so to produce beans before they are killed by frost. Agronomists have selected plants that are day-neutral so they can flower regardless of the amount of daylight received, allowing for a much longer cropping period. 'Moonlight,' introduced in 2011 by Tozer Seeds, was one of the first bean cultivars to result from crosses between French and runner bean varieties.

The rice bean (*Vigna gracilicaulis*) comes from tropical and subtropical Asia. It is a scrambling annual or perennial with yellow flowers and small edible beans. Domestication is believed to have occurred in Southeast Asia and there are a large number of different forms grown in the region. The seed colour is usually red or yellow. It is regarded as a minor food crop and is primarily used as fodder for livestock. It may be grown as a mixed crop along with maize, sorghum, or cowpea.

Found throughout the Indian Subcontinent and across to China, the moth bean (*Vigna aconitifolia*) is a creeping annual which grows approximately 40 cm (15.75″) high. It has hairy, densely-packed branches and yellow flowers which develop into brown pods holding four to nine seeds inside. Moth beans are very small and brownish in colour, with a creamy-coloured interior. They are similar in taste to mung beans but have a nuttier flavour. Also known as matki, dew bean, or Turkish gram, it is a drought-resistant plant, commonly grown in arid and semi-arid regions and valued for its ability to combat soil erosion.

The tepary bean (*Phaseolus acutifolius*) is native to the southwestern United States and Mexico where it grows in desert and semi-desert conditions. It is an annual that climbs or sprawls with stems up to 4 metres (13′) long. Water is required for germination but once established the plants are very drought tolerant. They have been grown by indigenous peoples for thousands of years. The beans vary in size and can be many different colours.

Broad beans

The broad bean (*Vicia faba*), also known as the fava bean, faba bean, or Celtic bean, is thought to be native to Palestine but is one of the most ancient of all cultivated plants and has spread around much of the world. The term 'broad bean' is typically used for large-seeded cultivars grown for human food, while horse bean, field bean and tick bean refer to cultivars with smaller, harder seeds commonly used for animal feed. The smaller seeds generally have a stronger flavour

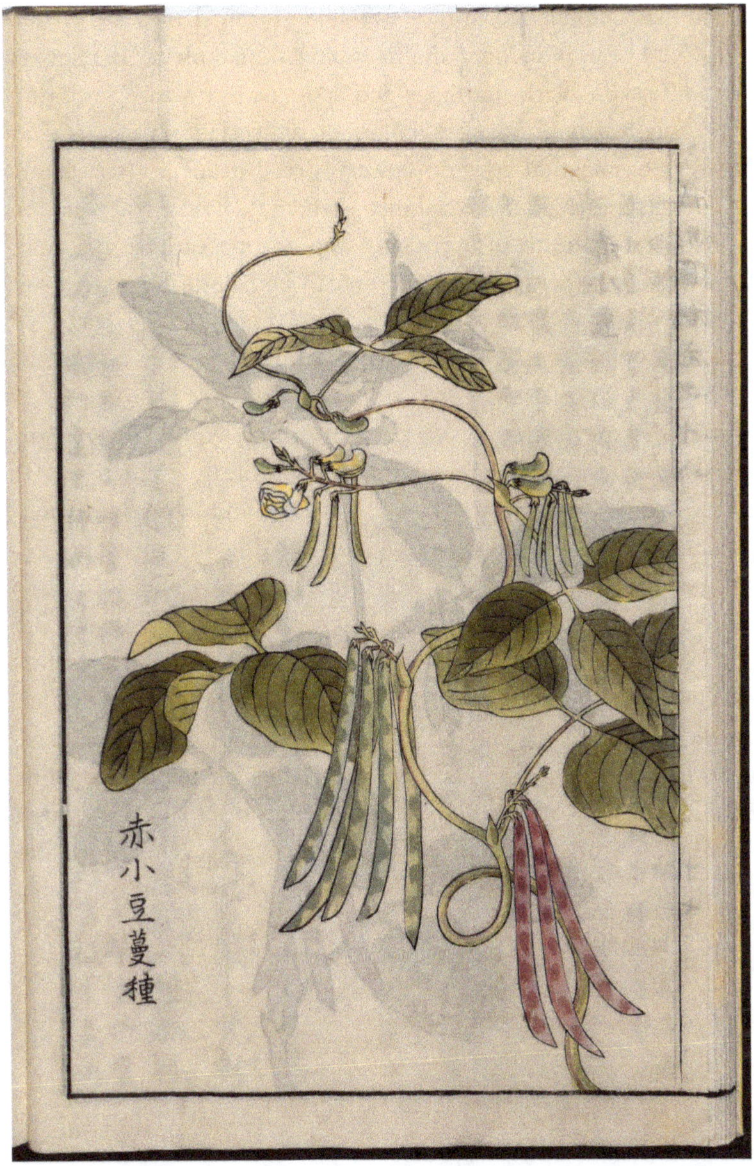

Fig. 7. Rice bean illustration from the Japanese agricultural encyclopaedia *Seikei Zusetsu* (1793–1804).

which may be preferred in recipes, such as ful medames and falafel. The broad bean is an erect, non-climbing annual plant. The flowers are white with black markings and spots on the wing petals and often have a strong, sweet fragrance. An old cottage garden cultivar has very ornamental crimson flowers. Broad beans are very hardy and tolerant of higher soil salinity than most beans. They can be sown in the autumn to overwinter and give an early spring crop. Overwintering them as a cover crop can be helpful to prevent soil erosion.

Peas

The garden pea *Lathyrus oleraceus* (formerly *Pisum sativum* var. *sativum*) is native throughout the Mediterranean and across Asia as far east as Afghanistan. It is a climbing annual or sometimes perennial plant. It is a cool season crop and does not thrive in high summer heat or tropical climates. There are now many different cultivars, some form dwarf plants whereas others are climbers. The pods can be green, golden yellow, or purple. The field pea, (formerly *Pisum sativum* var. *arvense*) produces large pale peas which are well suited to drying and storage. These are the basis of pease porridge and the pea soups that have been such important foods throughout human history. Because some peas lack the tough membrane inside the pod wall, the tender pods with immature seeds are eaten. The mangetout/snow peas type have flat pods with thin pod walls. Snap peas or sugar snap peas have rounded pods with thicker pod walls.

Chickpea

The chickpea (*Cicer arietinum*) is one of 45 species in the genus *Cicer*. The term 'garbanzo bean' has been used in English as well as Spanish since at least the early-to-mid eighteenth century. The cultivated plant originated in the region of northern Iraq and Iran and has been cultivated for at least 10,000 years. Some of the oldest archaeological evidence, from the site of Tell el-Kerkh in modern Syria, has been dated to the early Pre-Pottery Neolithic period (ca. 8400 BCE). Most chickpeas are self-pollinating. They are annual plants with many different cultivars with red, white and black skins. Ceci neri, which has smaller seed and a dark, wrinkled outer skin, is grown in the Murgia, a rocky plateau in central Puglia, Italy. Black-seeded chickpeas have sometimes been used as a coffee substitute.

Cowpea

Also known as black-eyed pea or blackeye bean due to the small black 'eye' or hilum, the marking where the bean is joined to ovary wall of the pod, the cowpea (*Vigna unguiculata*) is native to Cape Verde and tropical and southern Africa. It is a drought-tolerant species and is widely cultivated in semi-arid regions of Africa, Asia, and the southern United States. Cowpea grows as a bush or as a climbing plant, depending on the cultivar. It tolerates a wide range of soil types and grows well in warm climates. Cowpea is a fast-growing crop, with some varieties maturing in as little as 60 to 90 days, allowing for multiple harvests in a year. The young leaves and immature pods can be eaten as a leafy vegetable. The cooked leaves contain more calcium and iron than an equivalent weight of the cooked seeds. The snake bean or bodi (*Vigna unguiculata* subsp. *sesquipedalis*) is also known as the yardlong bean as the pods are longer than those of the usual species, though perhaps not as long as the names suggest.

Fig. 8. *Vigna unguiculata* ssp. *sesquipedalis*, Seikei Zusetsu (1804).

Pigeon pea

The genus *Cajanus* includes 34 accepted species, 18 of which are indigenous to India. The pigeon pea, *Cajanus cajan*, is the only one that is widely cultivated. It is a short-lived perennial or small shrub with attractive red-veined yellow flowers. Seeds can be a range of colours including cream, grey, purple or black. The scientific name *Cajanus* and the species name derive from the Malay word *katjang* (*kacang*) which means legume. The English name, 'pigeon pea,' derives from the historical utilization of the pulse as pigeon fodder. Pigeon peas are also known as cajan pea, Congo beans, gandules, toor dahl, and no-eye pea; the latter being a reference to the lack of a hilum blotch on most varieties, unlike the black-eyed pea. There are two main cultivated varieties: *C. cajan* var. *bicolor* known in Hindi as 'arhar,' a large, bushy plant which takes between six and eleven months to reach maturity; and the short-season variety, *C. cajan*, var. *flavus* called 'tuvar,' which can reach maturity in just three to four months.

Pigeon pea is most commonly used to make dal. In parts of Southeast Asia, the seeds are used instead of soya bean to make

Fig. 9. Pigeon pea (*Cajanus cajan*) *Seikei Zusetsu* (1793–1804).

tempeh or tofu. They are widely cultivated in tropical and semitropical regions around the world. Grown as a glasshouse crop in the United Kingdom, it can reach 2–3 metres (6.5–9.8′) high and may live for around five years. The seed yield drops considerably after the first couple of years so it is often grown as an annual. The green peas can be used like fresh garden peas.

Lentil

Lentils (*Vicia lens*, previously *Lens culinaris* or *Lens esculenta*) are very variable, as indicated by the range of different names, including beluga lentil, brown lentil, green lentil, green lentil, le Puy, and red lentil. Lentils are thought to be native to the area covering Iraq across Central Asia to the western Himalaya. They are scrambling annuals or short-lived perennials, growing to about 40 cm (15.75″) tall. The pods usually contain two seeds. *Lens*, the Latin word for lentil, was given to describe a double-convex shaped glass and the lens of your eye, because of the similarity of their shapes to that of the lentil. The leaves of different lentil cultivars vary in size and hairiness while there is also a range of colour of flowers and seeds. Beluga lentils, named for their resemblance to beluga caviar, are black and almost spherical. Puy lentils have small dark speckled blue-green seeds and are prized for their peppery flavour and the ability to retain their shape in cooking. They are grown in central France as an appellation d'origine contrôlée that is also designated a Protected Designation of Origin name in the European Union.

Bambara groundnut

The Bambara groundnut or earth pea (*Vigna subterranea*) is named after the Bambara people who live mainly in the upper Niger region of Mali in West Africa and for whom the groundnut is an important indigenous food. The species grows from northeast Nigeria to South Sudan and may also be known as the Congo goober. It is an annual plant which grows quickly with a lifecycle often of just 120–150 days. A small, low-growing plant with lemon-yellow flowers, it is self-pollinated. The flower stems grow downwards into the soil and the pods are ripened underground, similar to the peanut. It is a drought-resistant species that grows best on light, sandy soils.

Vetch

The common vetch or tare (*Vicia sativa*) is an annual plant with long sprawling stems that can reach two metres (6.5′) in length. The leaves are made of between three and eight pairs of linear leaflets that culminate in a branched tendril. The flowers are usually bright pink-purple in colour but occasionally white and are pollinated by bees. Vetch is mostly grown as a fodder crop for horses and cows, although feeding them excessive amounts can cause colic. It can be cooked for human consumption as a green vegetable but again should not be eaten to excess. Bitter vetch (*Vicia ervilia*) is an ancient legume crop of the Mediterranean region. The tiny irregular grains, which resemble lentils when split, are exceedingly bitter and need multiple changes of boiling water before consumption.

Lupins

Beloved of cottage gardeners around the world, the garden lupin comes in almost a full rainbow spectrum of colours from the red of the cultivar *Lupinus* 'Beefeater' and orange 'Towering Inferno,' through the clear yellow of 'Desert Sun' and blue 'Persian Slipper' to shades of violet including 'Masterpiece.' Garden lupins are purely ornamental: their seeds contain high levels of toxic alkaloids. There are however several species of lupins that are widely cultivated for food. *Lupinus albus*, the white lupin, originated in Sicily and has spread around the Mediterranean. It was probably first domesticated in ancient Greece and the use spread to ancient Egypt where the seeds remain a popular snack. The large flat yellow seeds are often sold in brine as a snack food like olives. In Spain they are a popular bar snack known as 'altramuces.' Lupin beans can be ground into a flour, and this is widely used in parts of Europe as an additive to wheat flour for use in bread, pasta, biscuits, and other baked goods. The South American lupin (*L. mutabilis*) is grown in the Andes. It has a bitter taste due to the presence of alkaloids, including unusually high amounts of sparteine which is what is known as a quinolizidine alkaloid, also present in seeds of the leguminous broom shrub (*Cytisus scoparius*).

Fig. 10. Garden lupin, *Lupinus* 'Polar Princess.'

Most lupins are of the 'bitter' type that have a high concentration of alkaloids, including one specific to lupins, 'lupanine.' These are heat-stable toxins, so cooking alone will not get rid of them. They are however water-soluble and can be removed by soaking the seeds in several changes of water until no bitterness is left. In the 1920s, low-alkaloid 'sweet' cultivars were developed that did not need to be treated before cooking. The sweet lupin cultivar 'Dieta,' bred in the United Kingdom, is bitter-free and said to grow well in the warmer southeastern regions of the country, although trials led by Garden Organic were not very successful.

Minor crops

Hyacinth Bean

Linnaeus included the hyacinth bean or dolichos bean (*Lablab purpureus*) in the genus *Dolichos* but it is now assigned to its own genus. It is native to sub-Saharan Africa, Madagascar, and India, where it is thought to have been cultivated as early as 2500 BCE. It is now grown widely throughout the tropics. A fast-growing, twining perennial climber, it will be killed by frost but can tolerate temperatures as low as 4°C (40°F) for short periods. It is a really attractive plant, ideal for growing in an ornamental potager or up a rose arch. The decorative foliage is often flushed with purple and the sprays of fragrant purple or white pea flowers are followed by edible green or purple pods which are variable in shape. The leaves can be eaten as a substitute for spinach and are used as animal fodder. When eaten as a pulse, the dried seeds need to be soaked and boiled to break down a trypsin inhibitor. As a perennial, it forms a large starchy root which is edible.

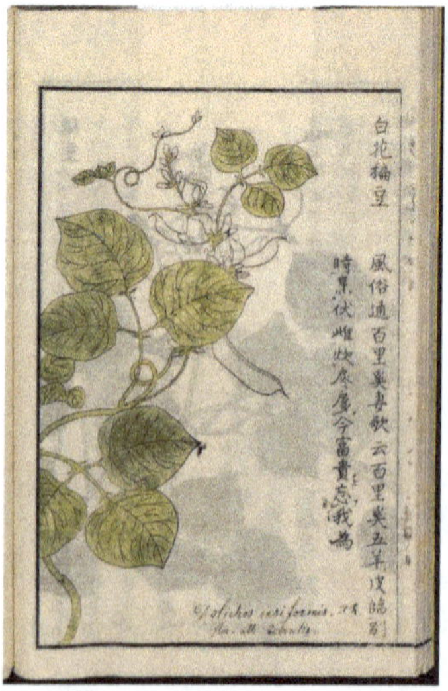

Fig. 11. *Lablab purpureus*, Seikei Zusetsu.

Jack Bean and Sword Bean

The Jack bean (*Canavalia ensiformis*) is an annual or short-lived perennial with both climbing and bushy growth forms. Probably native to South and Central America, it has been introduced in the tropics and subtropics worldwide. It is drought-resistant and rarely troubled by pests. It is used mainly for animal fodder and as a fast-growing cover crop to smother weeds in orchards. The pods are around 30 cm (12″) long and contain 15–20 beans which are white with a brownish mark at the hilum. The bean is eaten, especially in Brazil where it is called feijão-de-porco (pig bean), but it requires careful soaking and boiling to remove toxins.

The closely related sword bean (*Canavalia gladiata*) is believed to have come from eastern Asia but it is now also common in Saudi Arabia, East Africa, South Africa, and Madagascar. It is a tall climbing annual or perennial, growing primarily in seasonally dry, tropical areas. The mature beans contain high levels of harmful factors—including haemagglutinis (concanavalin A), protease inhibitors, hydrocyanic acid, tannins, phytates, and canavanine—and they require long-soaking and repeated boiling in excess water to safely eat them. The young leaves, flowers, tender green pods, and seeds are edible after cooking. In Japan, the young pods are processed into several kinds of pickles including fukujinzuke and misozuke.

Winged Bean

The winged bean (*Psophocarpus tetragonolobus*) from tropical Eastern Africa is a climbing annual or perennial plant also known as cigarillas, four-cornered bean, or dragon bean. It has edible self-pollinating flowers and leaves that can be cooked like spinach. The bean pod can be smooth or rough and the beans may be white, cream, dark tan, or brown. Varieties can be either short-day length plants or day-length neutral. Those grown as perennials form edible tubers. Mature seeds require long cooking to destroy the trypsin inhibitors and hemagglutinins.

Velvet Bean

The velvet bean or cowitch (*Mucuna pruriens*) notorious for the stinging hairs that coat its pods, is native to tropical Asia and widely naturalized and cultivated in the tropics. It is a vigorous climbing perennial or shrub with long vines that can reach over 15 metres (49′) in length. The new young growth is almost completely covered with fuzzy hairs which cause extreme itchiness on contact. The seed pods, known as devil beans in Nigeria, contain serotonin and the protein mucunain, which also cause severe itching. *Mucuna pruriens* var. *utilis* is a non-stinging variety. The beans can be eaten after soaking and boiling or fermentation to remove alkaloids. Unfortunately, the powdered bean, or something that purports to be that, is frequently sold online with numerous unsubstantiated claims that it can cure everything from nervous disorders to male infertility.

Horsegram

Macrotyloma uniflorum grows in semi-arid tropical regions. Its native range spans from tropical and southern Africa as well as the Indian

Fig. 12. *Mucuna pruriens* after a drawing by Miss S.A. Drake from *Botanical Register* vol. 24 (1838), edited by John Lindley.

subcontinent to Myanmar. It is a scrambling annual or perennial climber plant growing to a height of about 60 cm (23.5″). It can form a rhizome from which a new stem sprouts each year. The flowers are held in twos or threes between the leaves and are usually cream with a purple blotch inside. The curved pods grow up to 8 cm (3″) long and contain up to ten black, reddish-brown, or speckled seeds. Plants do not tolerate waterlogged soil. Archaeological legume finds from India indicate that horsegram was of widespread importance during the Neolithic period. It is still widely eaten whole, sprouted, or ground into flour in South Asian cuisine and also used for animal feed.

Tonka Beans

Tonka or tonkin beans are the seeds of the tree *Dipteryx odorata* (commonly known as cumaru, kumaru or Brazilian teak) native to northern South America. They are wrinkled black beans, resembling an elongated raisin, with a smooth, brown interior. They have a strong fragrance due to their high content of coumarin, a phenolic substance also found in cinnamon and sweet clover which can be a liver toxin. They are used sparingly as a flavouring in some desserts and cocktails but due to the potential for harm, sale is restricted in many countries. Selling tonka beans for food purposes has been illegal in the United States since 1954. They are however widely used in the perfume industry.

Yam Bean

Also known as jícama or Mexican turnip, the yam bean (*Pachyrhizus erosus*) grows wild in Mexico and Central America. Archaeological evidence from Peru shows that it was cultivated there around 3000 BCE. It is a climbing perennial that can reach 4–5 metres (13–16′) high, with tuberous roots which look somewhat like a turnip. They act as storage organs in the seasonally dry habitat in which it grows. It is frost-sensitive but small tubers will form as long as there is a growing period of at least five months without frost. In suitable climates the tubers can be massive: one grown in the Philippines weighed 23 kg (51 lb). There are two cultivated forms: jícama de agua has a top-shaped root and a watery, translucent juice; and jícama de leche, that has an elongated root and milky juice. While the root is edible either raw or cooked, the rest of the plant is extremely poisonous and must not be eaten—the seeds contain the toxin rotenone, which is used as an insecticide and fish poison.

African Yam Bean

The African yam bean (*Sphenostylis stenocarpa*) is native to tropical Africa and is considered an underutilized crop. Dr Nadia Radzman of the Sainsbury Laboratory, University of Cambridge has been working on a project to promote its cultivation as a multipurpose crop. It produces beans as well as edible tubers and leaves that can be eaten as a green vegetable. The tubers are higher in protein than the beans. Different landraces are being investigated to try to develop cultivars with reduced alkaloid levels and shorter cooking times.

Miscellaneous

Soya Beans

Originating in Eastern Russian, China, and East Asia, soya beans (*Glycine max*) need long, hot summers with full sun for optimal growth and yield. They grow best at temperatures between 22–35°C (72–95°F). The plants are erect, bushy annuals that sometimes produce twining stems. The small, inconspicuous flowers are white, pink, or purple and are self-fertile. They develop into dense clusters of short hairy pods containing two or three small rounded beans. These can be harvested at two different stages: when the beans are still green and immature as edamame beans, for adding to salads, stir-fries, and many other dishes, or when the pods are fully ripe and dry for mature soya beans. Some cultivars such as 'Black Jet' and 'Elena' are more tolerant of cooler weather conditions. Scientists have been using biotechnology to combine meat proteins with soya beans in order to reduce the environmental footprint of meat production and produce animal cruelty-free products.

Peanut

Peanut (*Arachis hypogaea*) go by many aliases including groundnut, monkey nut, goober nut, goober pea and pindar. It is not a nut. It is an unusual pea where the peanut pods develop underground. There are 83 accepted species in the *Arachis* genus but only the peanut is widely cultivated, although some of the others are used as fodder crops. *A. hypogaea* is tetraploid which means it has four sets of chromosomes per cell, whereas the other species have only two. The peanut is thought to have originated in Bolivia as a hybrid between two wild species, followed by chromosome duplication. Cultivation was well established in Mesoamerica prior to the Columbian exchange. It is an important oil crop with a total global production area of some 59 million acres, with China being the largest producer. Peanuts do better in warm conditions, but may do well in a polytunnel or greenhouse in less favoured climates. They have attractive, slightly hairy foliage and clear yellow flowers.

Carob

Carob or St. John's bread (*Ceratonia siliqua*) is an evergreen tree or shrub in the *Caesalpinioideae* sub-family of the legume family. The carob is native to the Mediterranean region and the Middle East but will survive in the United Kingdom with some protection in cold winters. It is a drought-tolerant species. Carob trees are dioecious, meaning that some individuals bear only female flowers while others have only male ones. Occasional hermaphrodites occur with both male and female flowers and these forms have been selected during domestication. Both kinds of flower have a strong, unpleasant scent. Carob was used to produce a sweet beer in ancient Egypt and is valued for its sweet edible pods which may be ground into a flour to produce bread in times of scarcity. The name St. John's bread was given because it was believed to have been given to John the Baptist to eat during his forty days in the desert. In Malta, the ripe carob pods are made into a syrup called Gulepp tal-Harrub which is used as a cough syrup and as the basis of the karamelli tal-harrub sweets eaten during Lent, when it is forbidden to consume more sugary sweets.

Indian Mesquite

Prosopis cineraria, known as Persian or Indian mesquite, khejri, or the Shami tree, is native to arid portions of Western Asia and the Indian Subcontinent. It is a small tree with thorny stems and small creamy-yellow flowers. It is extremely drought tolerant and can be used to combat desertification. The pods are used as a food in the Thar Desert. The tree is highly revered among Hindus and in 1730 CE, 363 members of the Bishnoi community were massacred while trying to protect the khejri trees that grew in their village from felling.

Liquorice

Liquorice (*Glycyrrhiza glabra*) is a legume whose roots, rather than the seeds, are eaten. It has sticky leaves and spikes of pale blue to violet flowers. The root is valued for its sweet, aromatic flavouring and is widely used in confectionery, drinks, and pharmaceuticals, although the glycyrrhizin compound which imparts the flavour can cause low blood potassium and muscle weakness if eaten to excess. It is a hardy plant and grows well in deep, well-drained soil. It is considered of historical significance in Pontefract in West Yorkshire which was once an important centre of liquorice cultivation.

Fenugreek

Seeds of the herb fenugreek (*Trigonella foenum-graecum*) were identified as forming the chief constituent of a large box in the tomb of Tutankhamen. The plant, also known as methi, is probably native to Iraq and Kurdistan but has been widely cultivated since antiquity. Its slightly bitter flavour is frequently used in Indian and Middle Eastern cuisine. The less common, smaller-seeded species (*Trigonella glabra*) is not as aromatic but will regrow after cutting, so is useful for extending the harvest period.

Tamarind

Native to tropical Africa but widely grown in Asia, tamarind (*Tamarindus indica*) is a tall tree with evergreen, feathery leaves. The tender young leaves are used in South Indian and Filipino cuisine. The brown pods contain a sweet, tangy pulp. Asian cultivars usually have longer pods containing six to twelve seeds, whereas African and West Indian varieties have shorter pods containing up to six seeds. The seeds are somewhat flattened and a glossy brown. Tamarind has a unique sweet and sour flavour and is used extensively in curries, chutneys, and bean dishes. In Madagascar, the pods and leaves are a favourite food of the ring-tailed lemur, providing as much as 50 percent of their diet.

FIG. 13. Tamarind pods.

Earthnut Pea

The earthnut pea, tuberous pea, or aardaker (*Lathyrus tuberosus*) is native from Europe to Siberia and in Iran. It is a common cornfield weed in Europe and has been cultivated in gardens in the United Kingdom since at least 1640. It can grow in highly saline soils. It is a perennial plant with pink fragrant flowers and edible tubers which taste something like chestnuts and are sometimes known as Dutch mice. Although palatable, the plant needs to be cultivated for two to three years to form tubers of a reasonable size so it is not a useful commercial crop.

Asparagus Pea

The asparagus pea (*Lotus tetragonolobus*) also called the winged pea, is a pretty annual plant native to the Mediterranean region. It is low growing and produces a profusion of attractive vibrant deep red flowers followed by seed pods that have four winged protrusions running down their length. The edible seed pods are said to resemble asparagus in taste, although the pea flavour is still distinct.

Hog-peanut

The hog-peanut or ground bean (*Amphicarpaea bracteata*) is an annual to perennial climbing plant, native to woodland, shrubby areas and moist slopes in eastern North America. It has a fascinating life-cycle, forming small pink or white flowers from late summer to autumn. There are two types of flowers: open ones which will cross-pollinate and closed flowers which are self-pollinating. The latter may be above or below ground. The open flowers develop into flat seed pods which dry and split to release their seeds in normal legume fashion. However, the closed flowers push themselves into the ground like the peanut plant and form round single-seeded pods which develop underground. The plant roots and underground seeds are edible once cooked. The Japanese hog peanut, known in Japan as yabu-mame, is the species *Amphicarpaea edgeworthii* var. *japonica*. It is native to East Asia, including Japan and China, and is commercially farmed in Japan.

Siberian Pea Shrub

Caragana arborescens, the Siberian pea shrub, is, predictably, a large leguminous shrub from Siberia, parts of China, and Mongolia. It is very hardy and thrives in most soil types. It grows rapidly and in some areas of the United States it is considered an invasive species. The yellow flowers are produced in early summer followed by pods containing small lentil-like seeds which can be eaten as a pulse and also yield an edible oil. The young seed pods can be cooked as a vegetable and have a mild pea-like flavour.

Moreton Bay Chestnut

Moreton Bay chestnut or black bean (*Castanospermum australe*) is native to rainforests on the east coast of Australia and to the nearby islands of the southwest Pacific Ocean. It is an evergreen tree with attractive glossy leaves and sprays of red and yellow flowers which attract birds, bats, and butterflies. It is often sold as a houseplant in the United Kingdom. Unprocessed seeds contain toxic saponins and will cause vomiting and diarrhoea but they have been prepared and eaten by indigenous people for at least 2,500 years. They must be carefully prepared by roasting, cutting up into small pieces, and leaching with running water for several days before pounding into flour and cooking as a form of bread. Unsurprisingly due to the work involved, the bean is rarely eaten as modern bush tucker today.

Pacay

Pacay (*Inga feuilleei*) is a tree native to the Andean valleys of northwestern South America and has been cultivated in Peru for millennia. The scientific name commemorates the French explorer Louis Éconches Feuillée (1660–1732). Pacay trees produce long pods that contain an edible white pulp whose smooth texture and sweet flavour gives the pacay its English name: the ice-cream bean. In Mexico, the trees are used to shade plants in coffee plantations and the seeds provide an additional income when roasted and sold as street food. The seeds should not be eaten raw. Unusually, the sweet pulp of the bean pod is not produced by the fruit wall but by the seed itself. *Inga* species occur throughout tropical America. *I. edulis*, locally known as 'guaba,' has pods that can grow to more than two metres (6.5′) in length. They are fast growing trees and resistant to fire and disease.

Milkvetches

The genus *Astragalus*, commonly known as milkvetch, contains over 3,000 species of which some species are edible, while others are highly toxic. Edible species include the ground plum or buffalo bean (*Astragalus crassicarpus*) which is a perennial plant with hairy scrambling stems. The immature spherical fleshy pods can be eaten, although the name given by the Dakota people *pte ta wote* (buffalo food), implies they may not be the first choice of vegetables for people. Some American species are known as locoweed or crazyweed due to a neurotoxin they contain that can cause swainsonine poisoning in grazing animals.

Interlopers

Any family can have its hangers-on and there are many so-called beans which are actually not in the legume family, notably cocoa and coffee beans. Cocoa beans are the seeds of the cacao/cocoa tree (*Theobroma cacao*), which is a small evergreen tree in the family *Malvaceae*. Cacao trees are native to the Amazon rainforest but have been spread widely by human intervention. Cocoa was an important commodity in pre-Columbian Mesoamerica. The fruit of the tree is a large pod up to around 20 cm (8″) long which has a thick, leathery rind filled with a sweet, sticky pulp in which are embedded 30–50 large, soft seeds. Although known as beans, these are more closely related to cotton, okra, and hibiscus than to leguminous beans.

The word vanilla is derived from the Spanish word *vainilla* which means 'little pod.' Vanilla beans were first domesticated in Mesoamerica, including parts of what is now Mexico, and were probably used to sweeten the taste of cocoa before the introduction of sugar. Although the pods look similar to some true legumes, all vanilla species are orchids.

Coffee plants are members of the large madder family, known as the *Rubiaceae* that contains other important plants such as *Cinchona*, used to make quinine, and the fragrant *Gardenia*. There are over 130 species in the genus *Coffea* of which two—*C. arabica*, native to eastern South Sudan, southwestern Ethiopia, and northern Kenya; and *C. canephora* var. *robusta* that grows wild from western tropical Africa to South Sudan and northern Angola—account for the majority of the world's coffee production. The trees produce edible red, yellow, or purple fruits, often referred to as coffee cherries, which each contain two seeds, known as the coffee beans.

The starry, feather-edged, white flowers of bogbeans are one of the most charming springtime sights in ponds, fens, bogs, and marshes throughout the northern hemisphere. The bogbean (*Menyanthes trifoliata*) is so-named because its leaves look like those of broad beans. The seed pods of the plant do not actually look like beans at all.

The New Guinea bean (*Lagenaria siceraria*) is not from New Guinea, nor is it a bean. It is in fact a climbing edible gourd/squash native to tropical Africa. Also known as the calabash or bottle gourd, it was one of the first plants to be domesticated by humans and has spread across the world due to its value not just for food but also for use as containers.

The bush bean (*Vincetoxicum lineare*) is a native Australian climber that has been an important food source for the indigenous people of Central Australia who have foraged for this bean for tens of thousands of years. It grows primarily in desert or dry shrubby habitats, producing slender, twining stems with thin leaves and delicate pinkish-brown flowers. The whole of the plant is eaten, particularly the green bean-like pods which can be up to 20 cm (8″) long. It is a valuable source of vitamin C. It is sometimes used in the making of bush bread. The bush bean is a member of *Apocynaceae* which contains many very toxic plants and excessive amounts of bush bean in the diet will cause weight loss in children.

It sometimes surprises people to know that the peanut is a pea, not a nut. To add to the confusion, the peanut tree (*Sterculia quadrifida*) is not in the pea family nor does it produce nuts. This deciduous tree is a member of *Malvaceae* and so, like cacao, is related to hollyhocks and the beautiful hibiscus shrubs. Native to the rainforests of New Guinea and Australia, it produces attractive scented flowers that are followed by vivid scarlet pods containing up to eight black-skinned seeds. Once the bitter-tasting skin is removed these are edible and have a somewhat peanut-like taste, hence the common name of the tree. To further complicate the issue, peanut wood does not come from the peanut tree but is a type of fossilised wood found in Western Australia. The name comes from the peanut-shaped markings that were formed by infill of the boreholes made in waterlogged coniferous wood by a type of marine clam. If the internet suppliers are to be believed, possession of a piece of peanut wood will assist you in channelling your inner vibrations.

Chapter 2
PYTHAGORAS AND THE BEAN

We lived very simply—but with all the essentials of life well understood and provided for—hot baths, cold champagne, new peas and old brandy.

Winston Churchill (quoted in William Manchester, *The Last Lion*, 1993)

A history of the domestication of legumes is effectively a history of mankind. The earliest humans were hunter-gathers and scavengers, foraging for food through the landscapes in which they lived. Hunting and gathering were the common means of subsistence throughout the Palaeolithic period which extends from the earliest evidence of stone tool use more than three million years ago until around 10,000 BCE. The controlled use of fire by early humans and the early food processing techniques of soaking and cooking plant materials would have enabled a much wider range of foods to be eaten. Cultural transmission of these techniques through the community was vital for human survival.

Evidence from Swartkrans, a cave near Johannesburg, South Africa, indicates the controlled use of fire emerged about 1.5 million years ago. In northern latitudes, the ability to regularly produce fire is suggested to have developed sometime between 400,000 and

300,000 years ago, at which time Neanderthals inhabited wide parts of Europe and Western Asia and may have co-existed with early modern humans. Fire was used to cook a variety of plant foods, including grains and legumes, so they could be used in the diet to supplement foods of animal origin, such as meat, fish, insects, snails, and eggs. Cooking is a vital preparation for many foods to ensure that they are palatable and safe to eat. It breaks down tough tissues making them easier to chew and alters the flavour and texture of food. Heat helps with the gelatinization of starches and caramelises sugars. It reduces any bacterial contamination and parasite load in meat and carrion and helps break down some of the anti-nutritional factors found in many plants—such as phytates, tannins and lectins—which would otherwise interfere with the absorption of nutrients.

Pulses could be cooked before the invention of pottery, either whole or first ground into flour. They could be baked or roasted on hot coals or in a sand/earth oven, made simply by lining a pit with stones, clay, or compacted earth. They could also be boiled in hide bags suspended over a fire or using pot-boiling stones, although maintaining a boiling temperature for a sufficient time to deactivate toxins would have been difficult. However, the introduction of heat-resistant ceramics allowed seeds to be boiled for prolonged periods, considerably expanding the range of pulses that could be safely eaten. In 2012 the journal *Science* announced the discovery of the earliest pottery yet known anywhere in the world at Xianren, a cave in Jiangxi Province, China. This was dated by radiocarbon analysis to between 20,000 and 19,000 years ago. In North Africa pottery has been found from around 12,000 years ago.

Examining pottery can provide a surprising amount of information on many aspects of human life, revealing details about human migration by comparing and contrasting pottery types from different sites to follow population movements and determine trade networks. The regular use of pottery typically implies a more sedentary life because pottery is often heavy and fragile, making it less suitable for fully nomadic people. Styles of pottery and any decorative patterns or motifs can also suggest details about a society's aesthetics and symbolism. Modern analytical methods allow the identification of remaining organic residues on even small pottery shards so that archaeologists can learn more about the kinds of food that were prepared or stored. Analysis of the carbon isotope ratios of oily residues left in over 100 broken pieces of ceramic material from archaeological sites at the Takarkori rock shelter and the Uan Afuda cave in the Libyan Sahara found that the pots were used to process a wide variety of vegetation, including aquatic plants.

Hunter-gatherers would have harvested the wild ancestors of the so-called 'founder crops,' those grown by early farming communities, for millennia before they were domesticated. Wild lentil species and bitter vetch were used as foodstuffs by the Mesolithic inhabitants of Franchthi Cave in the Argolic Gulf of Greece. Evidence from the Uzzo Cave on the island of Sicily shows that wild legumes including peas and other *Lathyrus* species were eaten at the time of the Mesolithic-Neolithic transition. At Tell Abu Hureyra, an archaeological site in the Upper Euphrates valley in Syria, the Epipaleolithic levels contain the seeds of many wild plant species including the grains of wild grasses and leguminous seeds such as lentils and some vetches, as well as the small seeds of clovers of the genus *Trifolium*. At Mureybet in northern Syria, the seeds of lentils, vetches, and astragalus species were found along with grains of wild cereals. The inhabitants of the region at the time were nomadic hunter-gatherers who generally lived in small, seasonal camps rather than permanent villages.

The Fertile Crescent is a term coined by Egyptologist James Henry Breasted (1865–1935) to refer to the crescent-shaped region of Western Asia formed by the Tigris and Euphrates rivers and the Mediterranean Sea. It stretches from northern Egypt through Israel, Palestine, and Jordan and across to the shores of the Persian Gulf. When the first human migrants were leaving Africa, the Fertile Crescent would have been an open landscape of rich grasslands and lush marshes with abundant animals, including gazelle and antelope, and a varied plant life. This region was the site of great agricultural innovations and gave rise to some of the world's earliest civilizations. Legumes are among the most common plant remains uncovered by archaeological excavations in the region from Middle Palaeolithic sites (about 60,000 to 50,000 years old), indicating that they were frequently eaten during that era.

Archaeological evidence can give some tantalising indications of the long use of pulses and how they have been domesticated. New techniques using stable isotope analysis of bone and the calculus that accumulates on teeth are enabling scientists working in the field of human bioarchaeology to develop some understanding of the lives and dietary habits of individual prehistoric people. Work at sites in the Azraq Basin and the marshlands of Jordan has revealed evidence of complex sociocultural behaviours and elaborate mortuary practices among hunter-gatherers. Researchers working on the Epipaleolithic foragers in Azraq even found one grave that includes a human buried together with a fox, suggesting a close emotional or symbolic relationship between humans and foxes prior to the first domestication of the dog.

Domestication is the process whereby wild plants and animals are selected and bred by people over progressive generations to promote favoured traits and adapt them for human use, a process which can lead to evolutionary change. Although the individuals of any plant species will naturally share most general characteristics, there will be many natural variations among those individuals. Early farmers would have selected plants with the most desirable characteristics, choosing the more palatable vegetables over their bitter wild ancestors and selecting for those which gave higher yields, large-sized grains, pods that did not rapidly scatter their seeds, and so on. Of course, those less-desirable traits, like bitter flavours and having seeds that spontaneously shatter, do favour the survival of the wild plants, so cultivated plants often become more vulnerable to insect predators and environmental stresses.

A degree of natural selection will also occur, imposed by their geographical locality and immediate environment. Although selection for a particular environment means that domesticated plants should flourish in the conditions where they are raised, they may perform less well if they are taken to new locations due to migration or trade. Over time, the offspring of introduced plants acquire new characteristics that enable them to better adapt to their new surroundings. This process produces diverse cultivars of crops known as landraces, each being adapted to the specific soils, weather patterns, and seasonal variations in day length found where they are grown.

Of course, domestication is not a one-sided process. In domesticating plants man changed them from their wild ancestors. If you plant a crop you have to tend it and if you want to plant the same crop next year, you have to save seed and have somewhere to store it until conditions are ready for sowing. Cultivating crops therefore meant that man had to make changes to his behaviour, but the potential rewards for those changes were significant. The Neolithic domestication of plants and animals provided the economic foundation from which emerged the cities and civilisations of the world.

Around forty species from the family *Fabaceae* have been domesticated as human food crops across the world, which is more than any other plant family. The differences between domesticated plants and their wild relatives are not always obvious and may be impossible to discern in archaeological specimens. The fava bean (*Vicia faba*) is certainly one of the world's most ancient crops. While the wild ancestor has not been identified with any certainty, charred legumes of a possible wild-type fava bean have been identified at el-Wad Terrace, a Natufian site in Mount Carmel, Israel. Radiocarbon dating of carbonised domestic fava bean remains discovered at three Neolithic sites in Israel's Lower Galilee suggests domestication of the bean may have begun as early as 8250 BCE. Seeds were selected for their thinner coats, which allows them to germinate quickly, an important requirement in dry conditions. Fava bean remains can be found in numerous archaeological deposits from the Neolithic, Bronze, and Iron Ages. Scientists believe that along with cereals, fava beans played an important role in spreading agriculture throughout Eurasia and North Africa. The earliest reliable evidence of the presence of fava beans in Britain is a Middle Neolithic pottery impression from the coastal site at Ogmore, Glamorgan and they are frequently found at sites from the Middle Bronze Age (around 1500 BCE) onward, particularly in southern England.

Peas and lentils are thought to have been domesticated simultaneously with wheat and barley, prior to 6000 BCE. Bitter vetch, chickpeas, and the grass pea (*Lathyrus sativus*) were probably also farmed early. DNA analysis has shown that domesticated lentils are most closely related to the wild *Lens culinaris* ssp. *orientalis* (now *Vicia lens*) which originated in Kurdish Asia (northern Iraq, southeastern Turkey and northeastern Syria). The earliest clearly-domesticated lentils were found at the site of Tepe Sabz in Iran and date to 5500–5000 BCE. Excavations at Gurga Chiya in the Shahrizor plain, Iraqi Kurdistan have turned up large quantities of lentils. A significant cache of lentils was found in a private house, suggesting that this was a valuable crop belonging to an industrious farming family rather than a resource for the wider community. The cache possibly represents an accumulation of private wealth and the beginnings of social inequality. Lentils have been reported by the botanist and ethnographer Georg August Schweinfurth (1836–1925) from among the funeral offerings in a 12th dynasty (2,200–2,400 BC) tomb at Dra' Abu el-Naga on the Nile's west bank in Thebes, Egypt.

Excavations at the Dra' Abu el-Naga site in 2017 unearthed a small funerary garden measuring 3 by 2.2 metres (9.8 × 7′). It was made of river silt strengthened with a layer of white lime mortar. The interior is mostly divided into a grid of 23 squares each of roughly 30 cm (11.8″) squares and separated by low silt walls. Each square served as an individual small planting bed with walls helping to retain water, an important feature in arid environments. Archaeo-botanists have so far identified coriander and a type of melon seeds from the garden and noted that a tamarisk was growing in the centre which would have provided some welcome shade. Similar 'square foot gardens,' also known as 'waffle gardens,' for food production are documented in the mastaba of Mereruka, a powerful official and son-in-law of King Teti, in Saqqara, Egypt from around 2300 BCE. The depictions in Meruka's mastaba have many similarities to the cultivation system used by the indigenous Zuni Pueblo in New Mexico, USA.

Domesticated chickpea originated in the region of northern Iraq to Iran. Some of the oldest archaeological evidence comes from the site of Tell el-Kerkh, in modern Syria, dating back to the early Pre-Pottery Neolithic period. The chickpea was probably introduced to Egypt during the 18th Dynasty (1550–1292 BCE) at the beginning of the New Kingdom. It was known as *hr bek*, the falcon-faced bean, probably because the protruding part of the seed was thought to resemble a falcon's beak. Howard Carter's notes on the botanical specimens found in the tomb of Tutankhamen record a basket of chickpeas given to sustain the pharaoh in the afterlife and a large box containing fenugreek seeds, spikelets of emmer wheat, some barley, and a few lentils. The common pea was a minor crop in Egypt but the British Egyptologist and botanist Percy Edward Newberry (1869–1949), recorded specimens found by Sir Flinders Petrie (1853–1942) in tombs in Hawara. These had smaller seeds than modern peas. A sample collected at the pyramid town of Lahun by Petrie in 1889–90 is now held at the National Museums Liverpool, World Museum.

While the archaeological evidence is obviously important in helping to identify food eaten by early people, the preservation of such evidence is very patchy. Some help with understanding the early domestication of food crops can be provided by specialists in the field of historical linguistics. In India, for example, archaeological finds of pigeon peas dating to about the fourteenth century BCE have been found at the Neolithic site of Sanganakallu in Bellary in eastern Karnataka, where the cultivation of African domesticated plants like pearl millet, finger millet, and hyacinth bean have also been uncovered. Historical linguistic data suggests the pigeon pea diverged into long-season arhar and short-season tuar types early in prehistory, over 3,700 years ago. The arhar types are regarded as more primitive and closer to the common ancestor. From India the pigeon pea is thought to have made its way to Africa as part of the Bronze Age trade that allowed cross-cultural exchange of resources and agricultural products. Seeds have been found in Egyptian tombs dating to around 2200 BCE. From eastern Africa, cultivation spread west and south through the continent, before reaching the Americas around the seventeenth century CE by means of the transatlantic slave trade.

The soya bean was probably domesticated in several different locations in East Asia, giving rise to erect bushy plants and seeds with a yellow seed coat rather than black. Evidence for domestication in the eastern half of north China occurs around the eleventh century BCE. The ancient character for soya bean (*shu*) appeared on four early Zhou dynasty (ca. 1046–771 BCE) bronze vessels, suggesting that the plant was already of some significance at the time. Soya beans were considered one of the five sacred grains in ancient China along with rice, wheat, foxtail millet, and proso millet. Radiocarbon-dated charred soya bean seeds indicate selection leading to increased seed sizes in Japan by the Middle Jomon period and in Korea by the Early Mumun period.

Genetic studies of the adzuki bean DNA have shown evidence of plant domestication by the Jōmon people in Japan. Hunting and fishing were important during the Early Jōmon period (5000–3520 BCE) but so were plants. The native plants growing around their settlements were managed and selected forms from the wild adzuki were developed. People also grew non-native plants introduced by trade. In a study of Neolithic hunter-gatherers around Lake Baikal in Russia, analysis shows that the area over which they foraged was less than might be expected, but burial goods indicated a very large-scale trade network including links between the island of Hokkaidō in northern Japan and Lake Baikal. The Ainu people, who mostly live on Hokkaidō today, once also inhabited southeastern Russia including most of the Kuril Islands. In the late sixteenth century CE, the Japanese Matsumae clan were given control of the southwestern corner of Hokkaidō, around present-day Matsumae, and were charged with defending it from the Ainu people. Fines were imposed on any Ainu cultivating crops on Matsumae lands and, despite episodes of famine, they were manipulated by being told that if they planted too many crops, the plague deities would become angry and spread epidemic diseases.

The Caral–Supe civilization of Peru is recognized as the oldest-known civilization in the Americas, flourishing between the fourth and second millennia BCE. Their diet included domesticated squash, beans, pacay, and sweet potato. The common bean (*Phaseolus vulgaris*) is thought to have two independent centres of domestication in Mesoamerica and the Andes Mountains approximately 8,000 years ago. Domestication led to increases in seed and leaf sizes as well as changes in growth habit. Most of the common domestic traits were selected for more than 2,500 years ago. The nuñas group of common bean varieties, which are eaten after toasting, are mostly restricted to certain parts of the highlands of Peru and Bolivia. Dried beans from both genetic lines were taken to the Iberian Peninsula from the Americas in the early sixteenth century as part of the Columbian exchange and from there distributed to the rest of Europe.

On arrival in the Caribbean in 1492, Christopher Columbus noted the indigenous peoples of the Caribbean growing crops that were different to those grown in Europe. The explorers observed root crops, maize, squash, and beans (*Phaseolus* species) and in Columbus' navigation journal for the 4th of November 1492 recorded that the inhabitants of Cuba *tienen faxones y habas muy diversas de las nuestras* (have cowpeas and broad beans more diverse than ours). The bean seeds are often attractively marked and are easily transported, so would have appealed to sailors and traders as a curiosity. Catherine di Medici took a bag of common bean seeds to Marseilles in 1533 as part of her dowry upon her marriage to Prince Henry, Duke of Orléans. They were widely grown in many areas of Europe by 1669 and probably introduced to Africa by Portuguese and Spanish traders through Sofala, Zanzibar, and Mombasa. The common bean became a major crop in the Central African highland areas of Rwanda and Burundi earlier than in other parts of Africa. While the Mesoamerican and Andean gene pools are both common in Africa, there is a higher prevalence of the Mesoamerican type in China.

The so-called three sisters—maize, beans, and squash—were the major staples of Central and North American agriculture. Typically, the beans referred to tepary beans or common beans. Traditionally the maize and beans were often planted together on mounds which improved drainage and increased soil temperature. Squashes were planted between the mounds. The cornstalks served as stakes for the beans to climb. The large leaves of the squash plants shaded the ground, keeping the soil moist and reducing weed growth while the beans fixed nitrogen in their root nodules. Studies have shown that the three crops grown together provide a greater total energy and protein than any one crop planted individually. Researchers have demonstrated that the combination of maize, beans and squash contains all nine essential amino acids for human nutrition.

The peanut, native to tropical South America, was widely distributed throughout South and Central America and the Caribbean during the time of the Spanish conquest. Peanut is thought to have been treated as a luxury food by the Moche people of Peru and was used in making chicha de maní (a fermented alcoholic beverage). Peanuts have been found as grave offerings in elite Moche burials at Pacatnamu and they remained an important crop after the Spanish conquest. The Spanish Jesuit missionary Bernabé Cobo travelled widely in Peru and noted in his 1653 record *Historia del Nuevo Mundo* that peanuts were eaten cooked and roasted, and that peanut milk could be used for medicinal purposes (similar to almond milk, which was widely used in Europe and the Middle East in the Middle Ages). Peanut was taken to Europe by the Spanish and spread by the Portuguese to their enclaves in Africa, India, and China whereupon it spread throughout Africa and Asia. In Africa, peanut became widely used in soups, stews, and marinades and is now an essential part of the diet in many countries. In some places it has become so much a part of the culture that people do not realise it is not a native plant.

Peanut butter, which is very popular in American diets today, was first made by the Aztec and Inca peoples. The pharmacist Marcellus Gilmore Edson of Montreal, Canada is credited with obtaining the first patent for producing peanut butter from roasted peanuts in 1884. The black American scientist George Washington Carver's (1864–1943) *How to Grow the Peanut and 105 Ways of Preparing it For Human Consumption*, published in 1916, encourages black farmers to grow and market peanuts. The American government has also promoted the use of peanut during periods of meat rationing. In the United States, peanut consumption per person was around 3.6 kg (7.9 lb) in 2024, about half of which was as peanut butter. The largest consumers of peanuts globally are China, India and Nigeria, with nearly 50 million tonnes of *Arachis hypogaea* consumed worldwide.

Food Taboos

Food taboos in one form or another occur in most human societies around the world and often originate in ancient times. Researchers

FIG. 14. Pythagoras shunning fava beans.

looking at Early Neolithic diets in Britain have found that stable isotope analysis of human bone collagen indicates that the diet contained little or no marine fish. This is thought to be a major change from that of Mesolithic hunter-gatherers, suggesting that fish and other marine foods may have been seen as 'taboo' in Neolithic Britain. Taboos are different to individual food preferences and refer to the deliberate avoidance of a food item for reasons other than simple dislike. Food taboos are societal rules, generally imposed on individuals by members of the community through instruction and example during upbringing. Food taboos can lead to protection of resources, helping to utilise limited resources more effectively or may have a medical or food safety basis. Many however are seen as religious or spiritual in origin (e.g., kosher, halal, and Jain vegetarianism). Shared taboos may help members of any particular group to maintain their group identity, creating a sense of belonging to a community.

The Greek philosopher Pythagoras (ca. 570–495 BCE) from the island of Samos is most famous today for his eponymous mathematical theorem. In Pythagoras' day, Samos was a major trade centre with a reputation for progressive architectural practice and a lively festival culture. The writer Antiphon reported that Pythagoras founded a school in Samos that attracted leading minds from all over Greece but that he led a simple life of study, living in a cave. When he was around forty years old, he left Samos to travel to Croton in southern Italy, where he promoted a communal, frugal lifestyle. The narrative poem *Metamorphoses* by the Roman poet Ovid includes a fictionalized portrayal of Pythagoras in which he implores his followers to keep to a strict vegetarian diet. The French Renaissance philosopher Michel de Montaigne (1533–1592) used this version of Pythagoras' teachings in his essay *Of Cruelty* (1776) to express his moral objections to the mistreatment of animals. The English poet John Gay linked meat-eating with tyranny in his 1726 fable *Pythagoras and the Countryman*.

The word vegetarian to describe a person who abstains from eating meat was, according to the Oxford English Dictionary, first used in 1842. Prior to that time vegetarians were often referred to 'Pythagoreans.' The poet Percy Bysshe Shelley (1792–1822) was interested in vegetarianism and his first wife, Harriet, wrote in 1812, 'we have forsworn meat and adopted the Pythagorean system.' The Pythagorean system was unusual in that as well as avoiding meat, adherents should shun the fava bean. The painting *Pythagoras Advocating Vegetarianism* by Peter Paul Rubens (1577–1640) shows the somewhat doubtful-looking disciples of Pythagoras listening to him while naked nymphs and satyrs and exotic monkeys cavort among a profusion of fruits and vegetables. The vegetables include asparagus, artichokes, cucumbers, cauliflower, and a particularly luxuriant cabbage while the only pulses are the pods of broad beans scattered around and under Pythagoras' feet.

It is not known what Pythagoras had against the bean and even the Greek philosopher Aristotle (384–322 BCE) was unsure, writing that Pythagoras forbid fava beans, 'either because they have the shape of testicles, or because they resemble the gates of hell, for they alone have no hinges, or again because they spoil, or because they resemble the nature of the universe, or because of oligarchy, for they are used for drawing lots.' Diogenes has a more prosaic explanation, 'One should abstain from fava beans, since they are full of wind and take part in the soul, and if one abstains from them one's stomach will be less noisy and one's dreams will be less oppressive and calmer.' According to the *Natural History* of Pliny the Elder, Pythagoreans believed that fava beans could contain the souls of the dead. Modern commenters have wondered, however, if there was a medical reason for Pythagoras to avoid the fava bean. One of the genetic strains of the condition causing favism, in which eating fava beans can trigger a severe haemolytic anaemia, is centred in the Greek plains, Southern Italy, and the islands of the Aegean.

According to the Greek historian Herodotus (ca. 484–425 BCE) who travelled in Egypt, 'beans moreover the Egyptians do not at all sow in their land, and those which they grow they neither eat raw nor boil for food; nay the priests do not endure even to look upon them, thinking this to be an unclean kind of pulse.' However, evidence of fava beans found in tombs dating back to the Old Kingdom (around 2686–2181 BCE), suggests that they were certainly valued at that time and fava beans continue to be of great importance in the Egyptian diet today.

Pulses were grown and appreciated for a variety of purposes during the Roman period in Italy. The fourth of the Eclogues of Virgil (Publius Virgilius Maro, 70–19 BCE) written in 37 BCE, addressed a newborn baby:

'On thee, child, everywhere shall earth, untilled,
Show'r her first baby-offerings, vagrant stems
Of ivy, foxglove, and gay briar, and bean.'

One of the more modest houses preserved in southeast Pompeii had a garden with grape vines, four large widely-spaced trees, and a number of smaller orchard trees. Carbonized fava beans have been found there, suggesting that vegetables and herbs would have been grown among the trees. The fifth book in the collection of Roman recipes *De re culinarian*, reputed to have been compiled

Fig. 15. The fava bean with a caterpillar from the *Book of Flower Studies*, folio 32 by the Master of Claude de France (ca. 1510–1515). The Metropolitan Museum of Art, New York, object no. 2019.197.

by Marcus Gavius Apicius sometime in the 1st century CE, has several recipes for legumes, including lentils with chestnuts and a gruel made from crushed barley with soaked chickpeas, lentils, and peas. It includes two recipes for peas à la Vitellius, named for Aulus Vitellius (15–69 CE), a noted gourmand, who was emperor of Rome for just three months. One suggests cooking peas or beans then adding leeks, coriander, and mallow flowers. A sauce is added, made by cooking crushed pepper, lovage, oregano, and fennel seed moistened with broth in wine and oil, then finished with drizzled green oil on top. The second recipe uses a pea puree with egg yolks, broth, vinegar, pepper, lovage, ginger, and honey.

Roman veterinary medicine included a prescription for preventing illness in oxen that required 3 grains of salt; 3 leaves each of laurel, leek, and rue; 3 spikes of leek and garlic; 3 grains of incense; 3 Sabine herb stems (*Juniperus sabina*); 3 stalks of bryony; 3 white beans; 3 live coals; and 3 pints of wine. As much magic as medicine, the potion was meant to be prepared and administered while standing and only after the farmer had fasted. The Roman writer Varro (116–27 BCE) wrote extensively on beekeeping in his work *Res Rusticae* (On Agriculture). Honey was an important product, used not only as a food and preservative but also in many medicines. He advised that the hives should be set near food and water, and if there is no natural food, 'sow crops most attractive to the bees: rose, wild thyme, balm, poppy, bean, lentil, pea, clover, rush, alfalfa, and snail-clover (for sick bees), but thyme is best-suited to honey-making.' Varro was obviously familiar with the black-marked white flowers of the fava bean and thought that priests abstain from eating beans, 'because certain letters of gloomy omen are to be found inscribed on a bean-flower.'

Some Romans believed that the souls of the dead could be housed in beans. During the annual Lemuralia festival, which took place during the nights of May 9, 11, and 13, family ghosts were exorcised from the home. The head of the household walked around the house barefoot at midnight, throwing nine black beans while reciting the words: *Haec ego mitto. His redimo meque meosque fabis* (These I throw. With these beans I redeem me and mine). Any unquiet spirits were thought to then settle in the beans.

Peripatetic Peas

The Romans introduced many new foods to the United Kingdom including cherries, sweet chestnuts, cabbages, celery, and leeks. Some of the earliest-dated lentils have been of charred specimens identified in Roman sites in London and Kent. They were most likely imported crops from the Mediterranean region. When Emperor Constantius II had the Lateran Obelisk shipped from Alexandria to Rome in 357 CE, 120 bushels of lentils were used in the barge as ballast, but would have then been sold for food. A dish of lentils flavoured with sumac was recommended by Anthimus, a Greek physician and dietitian at the court of the sixth-century Merovingian king Theuderic I. Described as the first French cookery book, his collection of letters, *On the Observance of Foods*, are full of useful suggestions such as the recommendation to hang your peacock for 5–6 days before cooking.

Another Roman introduction was the pea which grew successfully across much of Europe and was mentioned by Charles the Good, Count of Flanders, as staving off famine in 1124. Famine was a real and constant danger in medieval times. The Great Famine of 1315–1317 was the first of a series of large-scale crises that struck most of Europe early in the fourteenth century due to sustained periods of bad weather with severe winters and cold, wet summers. The records of a local official at Kinsbourne in Hertfordshire recorded the flooding of pea crops in 1321. Life at the time was short and for most people it was a struggle to find enough to eat. The English royal family, who had many more resources than most, had an average life expectancy at birth in 1276 of 35.28 years. During the Plague years between 1348 and 1375, it was only 17.33 years.

Chaucer, who wrote *The Canterbury Tales* during the late fourteenth century, knew the pea as 'pease' and in its dried form it was the basis for traditional pease porridge. In his allegorical narrative poem *Piers the Plowman*, Chaucer's contemporary, William Langland (ca. 1332–1400) mentions other uses for peas, 'Had not Piers with a pease-loaf prayed Hunger to cease.' In medieval Europe, wheat bread and meat were often reserved as foods for the wealthy, who would also have enjoyed a range of fruit and vegetables. The Stonor Letters from the late fifteenth century give an insight into the daily food purchases of a well-to-do English 'gentry' family which included apples, cherries, beans, and peascods bought in season. The poor would have eaten mainly barley, oats and rye. Peas and beans were often seen as animal fodder and food for the peasantry.

'For what was baked for a horse was a boon for the hungry,
And many a beggar for beans glad was to sweat,
And each poor man was well pleased to have pease for his hire.'
(From *Piers the Plowman*, Passus VI)

Pulses are still widely viewed as meat-substitutes. In Ethiopia the field pea (*Pisum sativum* var. *abyssinicum*) is called dekoko, which means 'minute seeded.' It is also known as the 'dero-wot' (chicken stew) of the poor.

In the fourth century BCE, the historian Xenophon of Athens had noted that legume cultivation replenished exhausted soils. The benefits of growing beans to improve soil fertility was also recognised in the medieval period. Cultivation of beans and corn on fallow land is mentioned in 1328 in coastal French Flanders. Fava beans were extensively cultivated across northwest Europe in areas of reclaimed marshland because they can grow in brackish soils. In eastern England, large-scale field cultivation of legumes enabled the maintenance of an intense and productive system of agriculture, by enriching the soil and providing high quality animal fodder. Black peas were the main legume crop in fourteenth-century Norfolk with smaller amounts of white peas grown for human consumption. Beans were seen as a garden rather than field crop. The Martock bean, a variety of fava bean local to Somerset, was first mentioned in records as early as the twelfth century and is still grown there today. In his 1548 *The Names of the Herbes*, which focused on plants grown in Britain, William Turner comments that 'Faba is named in greeke Cyamos, in englishe a beane, in duche Ein bon, in frenche Febue. Beanes growe in al coutreis in pletie inough.' He was familiar too with lentils, reporting that, 'Lentilles are sowen in corne fields and grow as Tares do.'

It was not until the sixteenth century that a distinction began to be made between the field pea that was harvested when mature, dried, and stored over winter and the garden pea which was picked when still green and eaten fresh. During the Tudor period (1485–1603), sweeter tasting peas that could be enjoyed green as a salad vegetable were considered a delicacy for the elite. The agricultural writer and poet Thomas Tusser (1524–1580)

Fig. 16. Peas from Elizabeth Blackwell's *A Curious Herbal.*

refers to Rounceval peas in 1573 as those grown in the garden as 'dainties.' The name Rounceval (or runcival) peas was derived from the Abbey of Roncevaux in the Navarre region of northern Spain. They are thought to have been grown at the London Hospital of St. Mary Rounceval which was founded during the reign of Edward IV near to the present-day Charing Cross Station. They were a tall-growing cultivar that needing the support of pea sticks. Though frozen peas have been thought of as a modern development, green peas were packed in straw in boxes and stored, along with other summer delicacies such as strawberries, in the ice houses of large estates as early as the seventeenth century. In France, Louis XIV was extremely fond of peas, and they became a craze at his court. In a letter written by his second wife, Madame de Maintenon, dated May 10, 1696, she describes, 'The subject of Peas, continues to absorb all others, the anxiety to eat them, the pleasure of having eaten them, and the desire to eat them again, are the three great matters which have been discussed by our Princes for four days past. . . . It is both a fashion and a madness.'

In *The Description of Leicestershire*, William Burton reported in 1622, 'The whole shire . . . yeeldeth great aboundance of Peas and Beans, more than any other Country, insomuch, that there is an olde by-word of the same, commonly knowne to all men, Leicestershire bean-belly.' The parish of Barton-in-the-Beans (now in the parish of Shackerstone) was particularly linked to the crop. Somerset too was renowned for its beans and an eighteenth-century saying reported, 'Take a Martock man by the collar and shake him, and you will hear the beans rattle in his belly.'

The English poet John Milton (1608–1674), best known for his 1667 epic poem *Paradise Lost*, advocated moderation in eating and drinking but did not believe in a vegetarian diet, which he saw as a rejection of God's bounty:

> *'[. . .] if all the world*
> *Should in a pet of temp'rance feed on pulse,*
> *Drink the clear stream, and nothing wear but frieze,*
> *Th' All-giver would be unthank'd, would be unprais'd.'*

Farmers had known for millennia that crossbreeding plants could favour certain desirable traits but the English gardener Thomas Fairchild (1667–1729) was the first person to raise an artificial plant hybrid when he successfully crossed a Sweet William (*Dianthus barbatus*) with a carnation (*Dianthus caryophyllus*). He had religious qualms about his 'Fairchild mule.' At the time many people believed that all plant species were made by God at Creation and breeding new plants could be an affront to His design.

Charles Bryant (d. 1799), the Beadle of the Court of Guardians for the City of Norwich, was fascinated by the new science of botany and believed: 'All gentlemen then that travel with the public good in view, should previously acquire such a stock of the Linnaean system as will enable them to reduce plants to their Genera and Species.' He built on material collected by Hugh Rose, (ca. 1717–1792), apothecary of Norwich, and in 1783 published *Flora diaetetica: or, history of esculent plants, both domestic and foreign. In which they are accurately described, and reduced to their Linnaean generic and specific names. With their English names annexed, and ranged under eleven general heads.* He included 14 varieties of peas raised for table use including Golden Hotspur, Essex Hotspur, sugar pea, sickle pea, and Rouncival, as well as eight kinds of broad beans including Sandwich, small Spanish, and Toker.

The Augustinian monk Gregor Johann Mendel (1822–1884) viewed his own scientific investigations as a way of understanding God's creation. He was curious about how physical traits were transferred from one generation to the next and found peas to be a model system because he could easily control their fertilization by transferring pollen with a small paintbrush. By using pollen from the same flower, he could ensure self-fertilization, or he could cross-fertilize with another plant's flowers.

He found that self-fertilized peas showed characteristics that remained constant in each generation including height (whether plants were tall or short), seed shape (smooth or winkled), and pea colour (green or yellow). However, when a yellow pea was crossed with a green pea their offspring always produced yellow seeds

FIG. 17. Gregor Mendel.

but in the next generation, the green peas reappeared at a ratio of 1 green to 3 yellow. This showed that certain traits could be dominant or recessive and established many of the rules of heredity, referred to as the laws of Mendelian inheritance. Mendel presented his paper, *Versuche über Pflanzenhybriden* (Experiments on Plant Hybridization), which demonstrated the actions of unseen 'factors,' now called genes, in determining the traits of an organism, at meetings of the Natural History Society of Brno in Moravia in 1865. It was largely ignored by the scientific community at the time but was introduced to Britain in the early 20th century by William

Bateson, the first Director of the John Innes Institute in Norwich. Bateson coined the word 'genetics' and in 1910 the Institute became the first research institute devoted to Mendelian genetics in Britain. The Germplasm Resource Unit there now houses over 3,500 variants of pea.

Chapter 3
CULTURAL LIFE

But since he stood for England
And knew what England means,
Unless you give him bacon
You mustn't give him beans.

G.K. Chesterton, *The Englishman* (1914)

The English author and critic Gilbert Keith Chesterton (1874–1936), who wrote a moving essay on the delights of regional cheeses, understood the cultural significance of food. It is of course not just the English for whom food is an essential part of their cultural inheritance. Food is indispensable for survival, and so a preoccupation with food is a universal trait shared by people. Humans, like rats, crows and cockroaches are generalist feeders and are able to thrive in a wide variety of environments because we can eat a diverse range of foods. The foods we choose to eat are usually part of a way of life that has passed down through generations. The globalisation of food may have expanded the range and combinations of foods eaten and made us less responsive to seasonal change, but traditional recipes, cooking habits, and dining etiquette can still reflect the values and beliefs of different communities and are vital parts of our cultural heritage. The UNESCO Intangible Cultural Heritage list includes many food-related customs and traditions and recognises the importance of individual dishes to particular cultures.

This importance is illustrated by the way our food is represented in other aspects of human culture: pulses can be seen in paintings and legumes appear in literature. From the first through eighth century CE, centuries before the rise of the Incas, the Moche civilization of northern Peru flourished in one of the most arid areas in the world. Effective water engineering projects and the production of beans, corn, cotton, and squash allowed many communities to thrive with regional centres from the Nepeña River valley in the south north to the Piura River, near the modern border with Ecuador. The Moche are best known today for their monumental buildings known as huacas, such as the Huaca de la Luna (Temple of the Moon) at Trujillo which was built from millions of adobe blocks. Moche craftsmen also produced exquisite jewellery and mummy masks in precious metals and stones. On viewing the Peruvian gold items that were shipped to Europe and ended up in the collection of the Holy Roman Emperor, King Charles V in Flanders, Albrecht Durer (1491–1528) an artist and son of a goldsmith, wrote that he had never before seen such wonderful, heart-warming artistic things. The Moche crafted intricately decorated ceramics including spouted bottles and vessels in sculptural shapes depicting a wide variety of natural subjects such as human figures, animals, and plants. These ceramics have often been found as valued goods in burials.

Lima beans were particularly important to the Moche people. Representations of the beans on ceramics sometimes show them with spots and other markings in regular patterns, leading archaeologists to speculate that beans may have been used as amulets, tokens, for divination, or even as a 'pre-alphabetic' system. Beans were stored and carried in small, leather pouches made from llama hide. The archaeologist Gail Ryser has argued that although originally an essential part of the subsistence base for everyone in the community, the lima bean became restricted to use as a status symbol by the elite or in temple ceremonies associated with the Moche warrior class. Warriors are frequently depicted in Moche art in the shape of anthropomorphic lima beans armed with knives, war-clubs, spears, and javelins. A vessel depicting the assault of bean warriors, now held at the Art Institute

FIG. 18. Moche ceramic vessel depicting the Assault of Bean Warriors, The Metropolitan Museum of Art, New York, object no. 64.228.6.

of Chicago, has a stirrup-shaped spout decorated with lines of striped and speckled lima beans. The body of the vessel shows many heavily armed bean warriors, each wearing a headdress that ties under the chin and is surmounted by a crescent-shaped ornament. The slender legs of the warriors are shown in running pose. The lima bean therefore came to serve as an iconographic representation of the warrior, perhaps symbolising aspects of life, death, and rejuvenation. The raw bean is toxic but planting a single bean can give rise to many more. Both these qualities would be of value to the warrior class. Beans continued to be culturally important in Peru and in the 12th–15th century, copper ornaments in the shape of bean pods were produced by the Chimú people who succeeded the Moche.

In addition to lima beans, Moche art also featured peanuts, including a fascinating example of a ceramic vessel in the form of an anthropomorphic peanut playing a quena flute. Peanuts were commonly included as offerings for the dead in elite Moche burials. Ritual vessels with sculpted peanuts have been recovered from sites in the Nasca and Chincha Valleys on Peru's southern coast and peanut pod designs on headdresses frequently appear on vessels depicting supernatural beings. A golden parrot carrying a peanut in its claws was recovered from the grave offerings found in a repository at Huaca de la Luna. Archaeological evidence suggests that ceramic peanut pendants were created using moulds from actual peanut pods. The Lord of Sipán, first of several Moche mummies found in 1987 at Huaca Rajada by the archaeologist Walter Alva, was buried wearing a necklace with ten gold and ten silver beads in the shape of peanuts.

The peanut plant's habit of inserting its pods into the ground may have inspired its use as a symbol of the return to the earth of those who die, although some scholars believe that peanuts symbolised fertility with the pod representing the womb and the peanuts inside standing for babies. However, Moche symbolic ideology is complex and peanuts depicted in the clutches of copulating rodents or anthropomorphic peanuts combined with owls and other birds or toads may be linked with agricultural production and the wish for a successful harvest.

In Christian iconography the two most significant flowers associated with Mary are the lily and the rose but many others have been used as Marian flowers to symbolise her virtues, purity, and role in the incarnation and redemption of Christ. The central panel of *Madonna of the Flowering Pea*, an early fifteenth-century triptych ascribed to the Master of Saint Veronica, shows the Virgin with baby Christ in her arms, holding a single stem with a pea flower and two pods. The contemporaneous Frankfurt Rhenish *Paradiesgärtlein* (Paradise Garden) painted on an oak panel around 1410 shows the Madonna reading in an enclosed garden accompanied by saints and surrounded by realistically depicted birds and flowers, and a small dead dragon. Saint Cecilia is holding a psaltery, a type of stringed instrument similar to a zither, for the Christ child to play and is wearing a wreath of pea blossoms which here are thought to allude to her chastity.

One of the most beautiful illuminated manuscripts of the medieval period, *The Hours of Catherine of Cleves*, was produced in about 1440 by an anonymous Dutch artist. Books of hours were extremely popular in the late medieval period and were intended for regular use, by ordinary people, to help them to structure their devotional life. The Catherine of Cleves manuscript, now in the Morgan Library and Museum, New York, contains images of hell, including souls boiling in cauldrons, which were not always considered suitable for a female reader. In contrast, a wonderfully domestic image of the Holy Family shows Joseph eating gruel in front of a fire, while Mary is contentedly breastfeeding Jesus. Intricate trompe-l'œil borders to the main images show realistic depictions of natural subjects including mussels, crabs, fish, birds, fruit, and flowers. A spray of peas is illustrated in the margin of a Passion scene and six pea pods with golden peas in a miniature with angels singing the Te Deum. The art historian Rosemarie Bergmann commented that these must allude to the special 'fruit of thy womb.'

Anne of Brittany (1477–1514) commissioned a book of hours which was illuminated between 1503 and 1508 by the French court painter Jean Bourdichon. It illustrates seasonal tasks such as treading grapes and sowing seeds and has accurate representations of over 300 plants, including native wild flowers as well as ornamental and food plants from the Royal Gardens of Tours. Most species get their own page and the roots and bulbs are often illustrated, as was done in herbals of medicinal plants. Several legumes are pictured, such as a pink-flowered chickpea attracting a range of beetles and butterflies. Most of the plants and wildlife depicted in the *Grandes Heures of Anne of Brittany* are realistic and easily recognizable, although the fava bean does have a pair of charming blue miniature dragon-like snakes curled at its stem.

The images in the *Book of Flower Studies* by the Master of Claude de France, painted around 1510–1515 would have been used as exemplars by the artists working on commissions linked to Queen Claude of France (1499–1524), who was the eldest daughter of Anne of Brittany and King Louis XII of France. The flowers included in this book were not necessarily chosen for their symbolism or as examples of medicinal herbs but were gathered through the year and painted to record their beauty. Folio 32 (see figure 19) depicts a pea in flower with two fruiting pods and a darter dragonfly, while

FIG. 19. Peas from the *Book of Flower Studies*, folio 32 by the Master of Claude de France (ca. 1510–1515). The Metropolitan Museum of Art, New York, object no. 2019.197.

Folio 39 (see figure 15) shows a fava bean with flowers and pods and a fairly chunky caterpillar.

De historia stirpium commentarii insignes (Notable Commentaries on the History of Plants) was written by the German physician Leonhart Fuchs (1501–1566), for whom the ornamental fuchsia was named. He was shocked at the poor botanical knowledge of many of his fellow physicians and thought it important for doctors to be able to properly identify the medicinal herbs they used. He commissioned illustrations depicting all the stages of a plant's life cycle, including the flowers and seeds. Published in Basel in 1542, the work describes nearly 500 edible and herbal species and was illustrated by Albrecht Meyer who worked from live plants. Fuchs included many of the new plants that were being introduced to Europe at that time, including chilli pepper, maize, squash, and tomato. Meyer's illustration of the common bean is thought to be the first depiction of that species in Europe. It was described as the welsh bean, at a time when *welsh* was understood to mean 'foreign.'

The common bean takes centre stage in *The Bean-eater* (*Il Mangiafagioli*), an early work by the Italian artist Annibale Carracci (1560–1609), who later became known for his large-scale religious paintings. Like his *Boy Drinking* and two versions of *The Butcher's Shop*, it is thought to have been painted in the 1580s when Carracci was in his twenties. All four are examples of scenes of ordinary contemporary life, demonstrating a clear interest in the humanity of his subjects. Carracci's *Bean-eater* looks at the viewer as if surprised to be interrupted while taking a spoonful of braised beans. The rest of his meal, including bread, wine, a bunch of spring onions, and a plate of erbazzone, a traditional Italian pastry stuffed with foraged greens, is spread on a white tablecloth. It is a simple image but intensely intimate. In looking at it you are sharing a moment with the bean-eater, even if he is not inviting you to share his beans.

There were many women artists active during the Renaissance and Baroque periods. Some, such as the Italians Sofonisba Anguissola (1532–1625) and Artemisia Gentileschi (1593–1653) and the French still-life painter Louise Moillon (ca. 1610–1696), were as renowned and paid as highly as their male counterparts. However,

Fig. 20. *The Bean-eater* (*Il Mangiafagioli*) by Annibale Carracci (ca. 1580–1590).

it is only in recent years that a new focus on female artists, their art, and their experiences has developed among art historians who had previously concentrated their studies on the 'Old Masters.' Women painters were more likely to produce still life floral images than other genres because flowers were seen as a more feminine subject. The famous Italian artist Michelangelo Merisi da Caravaggio (1571–1610) however pointed out that 'it took as much craftsmanship to paint a good picture of flowers as one of figures.'

Giovanna Garzoni (1600–1670) certainly demonstrated the highest level of craftsmanship in her work. Born into an artistic family in Ascoli Piceno in the Marche region of eastern Italy, she is thought to have first started to study painting with her uncle Pietro Gaia. Garzoni's first known commission in 1616 was in Rome where she produced illustrations for the herbal written by the chemist Giovanni Vorvino. She visited the Medici court in Florence between 1618 and 1620, where she may have met Artemisia Gentileschi. Members of the Medici family became Garzoni's main clients but she travelled extensively in Italy as well as to England and Paris. An admirer of Albrecht Durer, she owned a copy of his *Mother and Child with Saint John*. Garzoni painted portraits including the first known portrait miniature of a black person, the Ethiopian traveller Zaga Christ (ca. 1616–1638), whom she painted in 1635. She also worked on religious, mythological, and allegorical subjects but was best known for her delicate watercolours of flowers, fruits, and birds. The Italian abbot and historian Lione Pascoli (1674–1744) wrote that Garzoni could command 'any price that she asked' for her paintings.

Garzoni's *Still Life with a Bowl of Sugar-Snap Peas and Pink Roses*, painted in the 1640s with gouache on vellum shows an old ceramic bowl overflowing with peas in their pods. They are monumentalised by being represented on a rock in an open landscape and ornamented by an open pink rose with a rose in bud at the base. This brings an intensity to the humble peas in a similar manner to the simple painting *A Cup of Water and a Rose* created by Spanish artist Francisco de Zurbarán (1598–1664) ten years earlier. In the seventeenth century, observing nature was seen as a way of honouring God but intellectual investigation was also important due to the widespread interest in science. Painters such as Caravaggio strove for realism. His still life painting *Basket of Fruit* (ca. 1599) shows an apple with black scab and leaves that are withered or chewed by insects. Garzoni showed the same attention to detail. Her work, *A Bowl with Peas and Two Roses* (ca. 1655–62) demonstrates age spots on the petals of the greying rose and the pea pods display signs of insect or

Fig. 21. Broad beans as pictured by Giovanna Garzoni (1651–62), watercolour on parchment.

weather damage. *Hazelnuts with an Apple and a Pod* (mid 17th c.), which includes a careful study of a carob bean pod, shows an apple that, like Caravaggio's, has been infected with black scab.

Legumes feature in many of Garzoni's paintings. An early work features three pods of peas, four cherries, and sprigs of dainty strawberries. From the 1650s, *Chinese Vase with Tulips, Anemones and Jonquils, with a Fig and a Fava Bean* records a beautiful blue and white vase full of flowers, set against a black background and accompanied by a ripe fig and a single pod of broad beans. The *Old Man of Artimino* (1648–51) is a more complex image of a farmer and his comical dog watching over a feast of produce that includes a joint of ham, salami, fruits, a basket of eggs, an artichoke head, and a scatter of beans. Two wild birds have flown in, undeterred by the dead duck that forms part of the feast. Birds, butterflies, and other small creatures are common in Garzoni's work and may have had symbolic meanings. In seventeenth-century art representations of butterflies were often used to suggest the fragility of life, while the fly stood as a memento mori reminder of the inevitability of death and decay. Garzoni did include flies eyeing up the fruit in her paintings, but her bee flying away from the cherries in *Plate of Cherries with a Bean and a Carpenter Bee* (1642–51) is full of exuberant life.

Plate with White Beans (see figure 21), painted sometime in the 1650s, was one of the several works commissioned by the Medici family. It depicts a shallow dish of broad beans in their pods accompanied by two carnations and some bean leaves showing signs of damage. There is a further carnation and a scatter of shelled beans in the foreground. Garzoni used a stippling technique to achieve a grainy surface on the rock that the beans are displayed on. Carnations are edible and the old name for them 'sops in wine' refers to the practice of using the clove-scented flowers to flavour wine and other beverages. They were often included in portraits as a symbol of betrothal. In Flemish artist Joachim Beuckelaer's *Kitchen Scene with Christ at Emmaus* (1560) pink and white carnations are included in a basket of fruit and nuts. Another basket alongside contains a mixture of vegetables including broad beans and some turnips, whose snowy whiteness echoes that of a pile of carefully pressed napkins on the table. Beuckelaer (1533–1570) produced several paintings celebrating the richness of market produce, or perhaps showing off his talent for imitating the colours and textures of the vegetable kingdom while warning against excessive consumption. In his *Fruit and Vegetable Still Life with a Market Woman* (1564) early summer produce such as cherries and broad beans are displayed alongside autumn harvested crops including cobnuts and walnuts.

A less conventional use of fruits and vegetables can be seen in paintings by the Italian Renaissance painter Giuseppe Arcimboldo (1527–1593). Arcimboldo could produce conventional work when he chose, as demonstrated by paintings such as that of the Holy Roman Emperor Maximilian II of Austria and his family, but he is better known for his quirky portraits in which human features are made up of non-human parts. *The Jurist*, for example, painted in 1566 may from a distance seem a perfectly normal portrait of a lawyer wearing a black skull cap and a fur-trimmed coat but a careful look reveals his eye and nose are made from a featherless bird, his cheek is a chicken leg, and his mouth and beard are formed by a fish. *The Four Seasons* series uses plant materials to create human faces. *Summer* is depicted by a woman crowned with a garland of fruits and vegetables including cherries, plums, grapes, and an aubergine. Her eyes are cherries, her cheek is made of a peach, her nose of a cucumber, and her mouth and teeth an open pod of peas. She is wearing a dress made of straw, like that of a corn dolly. Arcimboldo was greatly admired by his contemporaries and in the early twentieth century inspired Surrealist artists such as Salvador Dalí, whose *Soft Construction with Boiled Beans (Premonition of Civil War)* (1936) anticipated the horrors of the Spanish Civil War.

Elizabeth Blackwell (1699–1758), born Elizabeth Blachrie in Aberdeen, was the daughter of a prosperous stocking merchant. She had been taught drawing and painting as a young woman and compiled and illustrated *A Curious Herbal*, published between 1737 and 1739, in order to raise money to pay off her husband's debts and to support their family. Encouraged by Sir Hans Sloane, the President of the College of Physicians of London, and Isaac Rand, the Director of the Chelsea Physic Garden, Blackwell took lodgings close to the gardens and spent several years sketching, engraving, and hand colouring more than 500 illustrations, including legumes such as broad beans, garden peas, and fenugreek for *A Curious Herbal.*

The still life genre has been remarkably enduring; first described in Pliny's *History of Nature*, in which he praises the ancient painter Zeuxis for creating grapes so real that birds would pick at them, the skill and artistry with which painters create works of beauty and mystery from things as simple as a plate of peas, continues to fascinate today. The Polish painter Mateusz Tokarski (1747–1807) is best known for his copies of works of other artists made while he worked at the Royal Gallery of Paintings but his *Still Life with Peas and Plums* painted around 1795, now in the National Museum in Warsaw, is beautifully observed with the bloom on the plum skins carefully rendered and the curling tendrils at the ends of the pea leaves delicately drawn.

Pulses also feature in other categories of art. French sculptor Edmé Bouchardon (1698–1762) created neoclassical statues for the gardens of the Palace of Versailles. He was a skilled draftsman and painter and produced two series of chalk drawings of the working people of Paris as the basis for a collection of smaller ceramic sculptures. These drawings, which include a scullery maid scouring a large pan, a knife grinder at work, and a man reading out the lottery winners, were later made into a series of etchings by the historian and engraver Anne Claude Philippe de Tubières entitled *Studies made of the Lower Class or the Cries of Paris* (1737–1746). *The Pea Shellers* (1737) shows two women sitting on boxes, heads bowed as they work, with a basket of shelled peas at their feet.

In the days before internet searches, crying one's product or trade in the streets was a useful way to promote your business. This was first recorded in the late Middle Ages and in the thirteenth century the Roman Catholic prelate Guglielmo da Villanova produced the oldest record of cried-out products. The early street cries give us an indication of some of the foods that would have been part of the diet at that time including Champagne cheese; pasties of meat, fish, or vegetables; warm broad beans and pea purees; and peas cooked with bacon. Many other artists produced Parisian city scenes such as

Fig. 22. *Pea Shellers* by Anne Claude Philippe de Tubières, comte de Caylus, after Edme Bouchardon, (1737) The Metropolitan Museum of Art, New York, object no. 53.600.588(12).

The Pea Sheller in the Marketplace by Etienne Jeaurat (1699–1789), a member of the Académie Royale in Paris. He exhibited regularly between 1737 and 1769, and was commissioned by Louis XV in the 1740s to create a series of paintings of mythological subjects. Many of his designs were used by the Gobelins factory in Paris to make tapestries.

Fig. 23. *The Pea Cart* (1788) etching by Thomas Rowlandson, The Metropolitan Museum of Art, New York, object no. 59.533.257.

Other cities of course had their cries. The English artist and caricaturist Thomas Rowlandson (1757–1827) was noted for his satirical images. Born in London, he was producing humorous sketches of his schoolmasters and fellow pupils before he was ten years old. He was a prolific artist and drew many images of the cries of London including *Milk O* (1820) which depicts a woman providing jugs of milk to two thirsty customers while a dog begs behind her. Rowlandson's image of *The Pea Cart* (1788) shows a man in front of a horse and cart crying his wares while a woman pours peas from a pail into the apron of her customer. *Cries of London, Fresh Gathered Peas* (1795) by English painter Francis Wheatley (1747–1801) shows a man and a boy standing on a cart. The man pours peas from a basket into the apron of a woman standing below. The English painter William Redmore Bigg (1755–1828) produced many small portraits in oil and pastel, and particularly enjoyed creating domestic scenes with children such as his *Black Monday or the Departure for School* in which two boys are sent off to boarding school. These were highly popular in his day with many prints being made of them. In *A Girl*

Shelling Peas (1782), Redmore Bigg depicts a young woman sitting outside her humble cottage with a ceramic pot on her apron and an overflowing basket of peas at her side.

Vincent van Gogh (1853–1890) primarily sought his inspiration in everyday life. As a young man, he had worked as an art dealer and took up painting in 1881. Van Gogh's early works consist mostly of still lifes and depictions of poor working people such as *Woman Peeling Potatoes* (1882). *Woman Shelling Peas* (see figure 24) is a chalk on paper drawing made in 1885 when Van Gogh lived and worked in Nuenen in the Netherlands. It illustrated a woman sitting in her cottage, lit by light from the window behind her, with clogs on her feet. She is shelling peas into a cloth on her lap with more to be done in the bowl on the table behind her. The drawing was sent by the artist for his brother Theo van Gogh. Camille Pissarro (1830–1903), sometimes called the 'father of impressionism' saw some of Van Gogh's work in 1884 and praised it. Pissarro's own *Peasants in a Field of Beans* (1891) with two women stooping over at their work, shares that appreciation of the hard lives that their subjects endured.

The artist and instructor Frank Stanley Herring (1894–1966) from Pennsylvania in the United States was known for his sensitive portraits of black Americans in Georgia. He produced the delightful watercolour *Laura Shelling Butter Beans* which depicts a young girl with a colander of beans on her lap and many more still to be shelled in the wooden bowl on the table beside her. In Japan, Itō Jakuchū (1716–1800) the son of a greengrocer, used plants including vegetables and birds such as chickens as his main subjects. His *Compendium of Vegetables and Insects* scroll (ca. 1790), 12 metres in length, depicts almost 90 different fruits and vegetables and over 50 varieties of insects and other creatures. *Bean Vine* (mid-18th c.), a simpler sketch of his, now in The Metropolitan Museum of Art in New York, illustrates a climbing bean plant and is paired with a poem by the monk Musen Jōzen, which compares him and his brother to the parts of a bean plant with the sword-like bean pod and the stalk coming from the same roots. This was part of a set of six paintings of vegetables which included *Peapods on a Branch* (mid-18th c.).

Pulses were not just painted but also carved from material such as wood and ivory. In the early sixteenth century there was a

Fig. 24. *Woman Shelling Peas*, Vincent van Gogh (1885) Van Gogh Museum, Amsterdam (Vincent van Gogh Foundation), object no. d0369V1962.

fashion in northern Germany and the Netherlands for tiny prayer beads, also called prayer nuts, carved out of boxwood. Wealthy patrons would commission tiny boxwood rosaries and miniature biblical scenes of extraordinary craftsmanship. Box, fir, and pine were the three trees mentioned in Isaiah 60:13 that would glorify the Temple of Jerusalem. As evergreens, they were considered emblematic of eternal life. Most of the surviving prayer beads are between the size of a walnut and a golf ball and were designed so they could be held in the hand to stimulate personal devotion. The Chatsworth Rosary (1509–1526) given to Catherine of Aragon by Henry VIII consists of ten small beads and a larger one or paternoster suspended from a crucifix. The paternoster bead has a hinge that opens to reveal a carving of the Mass of St. Gregory and the Adoration of the Virgin and Child by Angels. A captivating boxwood carving by a North German artist from around 1500 takes the form of a pea pod around 10 cm (4″) in length. It opens to reveal five little peas which can themselves be opened to reveal tiny carved scenes from the Bible on each half-pea.

The Anglo-Dutch sculptor and wood carver Grinling Gibbons (1648–1721), most famous for his decorative carvings in limewood, had a highly successful business supplying statuary and church monuments in wood, stone and marble. At one stage he employed more than fifty workers at his workshop. Many of his carvings include festoons and swags of fruits and flowers where pea pods are regularly featured. At St. James's Church in Piccadilly for example there are pea pods among the corn and fruit. An apocryphal story about the pea pods relates that the pea pod was Grinling Gibbons' signature and if the pea pod was closed, he was still waiting for his fee, whereas if it was open, displaying its peas, he had been paid for his work. The screens behind the altar at St. Mary Abchurch, the smallest of the London churches built by Christopher Wren following the Great Fire of 1666 however, include both closed and open pea pods, so perhaps Grinling had only received a deposit.

Originating in seventeenth century Japan, a netsuke is a miniature sculpture that was used as a toggle to attach items to a sash or belt. They can be made of many different materials but ivory predominated before the 1989 ban on cross-border ivory sales. The most common type is the katabori or figural netsuke which are small three-dimensional figures carved 'in the round.' Subjects are usually depicted in a very naturalistic manner and carvings that are pleasing to touch are favoured so they can be held like a talisman. Manju netsuke are either solid or made in two halves and are named after a type of rounded sweet dumpling filled with bean paste. Many netsuke are carved in the form of animals, plants, mythical creatures, or gods. One in the collection of the British Museum is carved as two bean pods with a purplish-green bean inside and another in the collection made of ivory, wood and metal has a bean pod and ants. The netsuke artist Rantei (active late-18th c. to mid-19th c.) was known for his intricate carvings, often depicting animals such as dogs and foxes as well as more complex subjects, such as the *Skeleton Astride a Skull*, in The Metropolitan Museum of Art's permanent collection. He also carved an ivory netsuke of a rat with a bean pod. Even if you are not a fan of rats, it is hard not to be enchanted by the miniature animal scratching his ear with a back paw whilst clutching the pod in its front paws.

Pulses find their way onto textiles and fashion items too. Peas were a popular motif on Tudor textiles with the twisting tendrils embroidered across clothing, cushions, and bed hangings. Exquisitely-knotted three dimensional peas added great textural interest. Until the end of the seventeenth century, the coif was commonly worn as an informal head covering by both men and women. Plain linen versions were worn by the working-class but more affluent women could wear elaborate coifs, often decorated with blackwork embroidery. A very lavishly embroidered version dating from 1575–1624 in the collection of the Victoria and Albert Museum in London used coloured silks in shades of green, pink, blue, red, and yellow with chain-stitched silver and silver-gilt threads. The front was edged with silver-gilt bobbin lace with spangles. The design was made up of leaves, roses, pomegranates, and pea pods. A contemporaneous textile surviving in a private collection was embroidered with Tudor roses, blue cornflowers, butterflies, birds, and caterpillars in brightly coloured silks and gold thread. The pea pods were stitched in detached buttonhole stitch and can be lifted to reveal little peas.

Some Tudor fashions seem ridiculous to us today and even to their contemporaries, many wearers of that shamelessly masculine item of dress, the codpiece, were the focus of ridicule. The word codpiece comes from the Old English 'cod,' meaning a bag or the male scrotum, and originally it was a triangle of cloth designed to close a revealing gap between the two separate legs of a man's hose. Modesty gave way to overt displays of masculinity and virility and the codpiece, stuffed with wool and sometimes even decorated with jewels, grew to startling proportions. The codpiece had fallen out of fashion by the 1590s but it was replaced by another trend, the padded 'peascod' doublet, thought to look like a pea pod ready to be picked. Like the codpiece it was seen as a symbol of virility.

The word peascod was used as a general term for peas in their pod. The Privy Purse expenses of Elizabeth of York from 1502 records, 'Item, to wif of William Greneweye for bringing a present of peesecoddes to the Quene, 11s.' Various spellings of the word including Peascod, Peasegod, Peasegood, Pescod, and Peskett were used as occupational surnames for street sellers of 'hot peascods.' Several early cookery books included recipes for sweet and savoury pasties formed into the shape of pea pods. In some cultivars of peas, the pods usually grow in pairs on the stalk, so they could be seen as symbols of the unity of two in one at marriage and the reproductive fruits of the union. An exploration by the historian Juana Green of handkerchief designs in the English Renaissance drama *The Fair Maid of the Exchange* (1607) by Thomas Heywood (1573–1641) shows that the pea pod motif could represent betrothal, marriage, and fertility. One of the main characters in the play, Mall Berry, decides to adorn her true love's handkerchief with pea blossom and a peascod, rather than the more usual rose or carnation, using these as emblems of her love. Like the strawberry-spotted handkerchief that was Othello's first gift to Desdemona, the handkerchief was a popular love gift in the Elizabethan era but also, in its role as a device for wiping away tears, it can serve as a signifier of sorrow and consolation.

The textile known as the Bacton Altar Cloth, from St. Faith's Church, Bacton in Herefordshire, has been thought to be all that remained of an original dress of Queen Elizabeth I. The remnant, made of silk and Italian cloth of silver, used dyes from India and cochineal from Mexico, and was embroidered in an elaborate floral design. During the medieval era, sumptuary laws ensured that people wore materials considered appropriate to their status as a way of maintaining the social order. Cloth of silver was reserved for members of the royal family. The Bacton Altar Cloth showed signs of the pattern cutting required for a dress bodice and it may have originally been a dress handed down by Elizabeth to her favourite lady-in-waiting, Blanche Parry, who came from Bacton. Skilfully embroidered, it is covered with delightful images of flowers, butterflies, and frogs. The main floral patterns, including a beautiful pea plant with flowers and pea pods, were taken from a design book, *Les Clefs du Champs* (The Key to the Fields), published in 1586. Smaller, more individual, and quirky images, such as the bear, are thought to have been added later by ladies of the court. These designs were taken from *Four-Legged Animals* (1594) by the Flemish engraver Nicolaes de Bruyn.

The charm of the pea pod motif has never really gone out of fashion. The French designer Hubert de Givenchy (1927–2018), known for his long professional relationship with Audrey Hepburn, opened his own design house in 1952. His spring/summer collection of 1953 included a quirky day dress with embroidered pea pod motifs. However, as the fashion industry becomes more environmentally-aware, the use of legumes could expand from motifs to fibres. Caroline Hyde-Brown works with the grass pea (*Lathyrus sativus*) at Norwich University of the Arts to create a sustainable biomaterial. She uses it to produce handmade papers and plant pots but suggests that further research could enable the fibres to be used as textiles. The artist and researcher Vivienne Schadinsky combines sustainable art projects and delightful works such as her Japanese-inspired paper and black bean sculpture with environmental storytelling and engagement. Her work had been on display during The Food Foundation's Bean Summit in 2025.

Beans as Beads

The wearing of jewellery is universal across human cultures. The earliest known surviving ornamental beads include seashells dated to between 150,000–70,000 years ago from Africa and the eastern Mediterranean coast. Beads have been made from a diverse range of materials including ivory, bone, human and animal teeth, and stones. The seeds of many legumes have been used as beads for jewellery and rosaries for thousands of years. To make a satisfactory, durable bead the seed must be firm, dry, and not prone to splitting. This means that ordinary edible beans are not ideal, as they are usually selected to have thin skins and split easily. Seeds are also chosen for their pleasant shape and appealing colours or markings such as the black and white 'Yin Yang' bean. The seeds of *Ormosia*, native to the tropical Americas, are so commonly used as beads that the trees are known as necklace trees. Children in Peru are given apotropaic seed bracelets (designed to ward off evil) and in Costa Rica wearing the seeds is said to guard against misfortune and bad luck.

Indigenous people from the Great Plains of North America wore seeds of the mescal bean (*Dermatophyllum secundiflorum*) in necklaces or sewn onto clothing to protect themselves from harm. The Tarahumara people of the Copper Canyon region of Mexico's Sierra Madre use the bright red or orange seeds of *Erythrina flabelliformis*, a small tree known as chilicote or the western coral bean. The brown seeds of *Cassia grandis*, the pink-shower tree, are used for necklaces in Central America. The snuffbox sea bean, *Entada phaseoloides*, is a woody vine native to tropical Asia. The sturdy brown seeds, which can be up to 5 cm (2″) long, can sometimes be found on beaches and are considered to bring good luck. They, like the largest and most common sea bean, *E. gigas*, can be hollowed out to make small containers such as snuff boxes. The kernel of *E. gigas* is often loose and rattles when shaken so they were sometimes given to babies and children as a toy. In Tonga, the seeds are used as ankle decorations for their traditional kailao dance as well as for use in an ancient game called lafo.

Saga, the Malay name for *Adenanthera pavonina*, originates with the Arabic word for goldsmith and in India the seeds have been used as units of weight for fine gold from early times. Also known as red sandalwood, the tree itself is used for timber and a red dye can be obtained from the wood. The shiny scarlet seeds were frequently used for jewellery or carefully hollowed out to serve as receptacles for miniature carved ivory animals for the tourist trade.

The nickernut (*Guilandina bonduc*) is a climbing shrub native to southeast Asia. The oval, flattened pods have a thick, spiny covering and contain two or three spherical, light grey seeds about 1 cm (0.4″) in diameter. The seeds are buoyant and durable enough to be dispersed by ocean currents. They are known to have floated for more than 30 years under test conditions. The related species *Guilandina major* has yellow seeds. The common name, nickernuts, refers to the use of the seeds as substitutes for marbles or in mancala-type board games and is thought to derive from the Dutch word 'knikker,' meaning marble.

The widespread jequirity bean or rosary pea (*Abrus precatorius*), also known as the bead vine or coral bead plant, has pretty, shiny black and red seeds which are used for necklaces and rosaries in many tropical countries. Dr. Gerhard Prenner of the Royal Botanic Gardens, Kew warns that its seeds contain the highly poisonous protein abrin, which is a plant lectin, related to ricin. Ingestion of a single seed can be fatal to both adults and children. Jequirity bean jewellery, and those made from other toxic seeds are not recommended, particularly if children or pets could get hold of them.

Superstition, Magic and Divination

It was not just Jack who believed that beans could be magical. Human societies around the world and throughout different time periods have searched for ways of predicting future events. The Oxford English Dictionary defines divination as the use of supernatural means to find out about the future or the unknown. People may look to the stars for answers, read the future in tea leaves, or use tarot cards for decision making. Ancient societies tended to class divination as a technical skill. The Athenian statesman Solon (ca. 630–560 BCE), one of the 'Seven Sages of Greece,' considered prophecy a *technē*, along with fishing and farming. Even today, with the wealth of scientific data available to us, such ideas can be remarkably persistent. Confirmation bias means that we tend to gravitate toward information that supports what we already believe, or want to believe, while the phenomenon known as emotional reasoning ensures that once we have a belief, we tend to cling to it, even when evidence indicates that it is untrue.

Favomancy is a form of divination that involves throwing beans and interpreting the patterns into which they fall. There are many variations on the theme. In Turkish culture the practice was known as *fasulye fali* (bean fortune) and was used to gain insights into various aspects of life, such as love, health, or fortune. In the Balkans, the ritual commonly used forty-one white beans thrown onto a cloth which was marked with a three-by-three grid. Practitioners claimed to interpret meaning based on the numbers of the beans in each individual quadrant. Persian literature includes references to divination by chickpeas. The large pods of fano (*Entada chrysostachys*) are used by practitioners of *sikidy* in Madagascar who are consulted over questions such as the best day to take a trip, plant a crop, arrange a wedding, and finding a spouse or lost objects. In Russia, favomancy was practised particularly by seers of the Ubykh people (who lived in present-day Sochi). In 1689, a horse-doctor called Doroshka was accused of sending 'a spell on the wind' to harm the young Tsar Peter and of reading palms and bean divination. The inquisitorial records of the trial of a 37-year-old widow named Antonia Bello in Mexico include a deposition from Leonor de Yslas describing Bello in an act of favomancy. He claimed that in December 1625 he walked in on a fortune-telling session in which Bello offered her neighbour Beatriz de Valdés advice on how to find a group of Portuguese slave traders who would sell Valdés a captive on credit.

Many religions disapprove of divination. The Bible states firmly, 'Do not practise divination or seek omens' (Leviticus 19:26). In Islam divination is considered a sin and an affront to God, who alone should determine what is to come. However, Keith Thomas argues in *Religion and the Decline of Magic: Studies in Popular Beliefs in Sixteenth and Seventeenth-Century England* (2003) that many divination practices bore a close relationship to the religious ideas of the period, 'In offering an explanation for misfortune, and a means of redress at times of adversity, they seemed to be discharging a role very close to that of the established Church and its rivals.'

In Sicily, fava beans are associated with St. Joseph because, according to legend, he answered the prayers of those begging for relief from a drought on the island. Rains came at just the right time for the fava bean crops, providing the people with the food they desperately needed. The beans are still carried for luck, particularly on St. Joseph's Day, March 19.

There is a long tradition of sea beans being found and treasured as amulets. They were worn on a string around the neck in the hope of averting witchcraft and the evil eye. There was a belief that the bean changed colour as it absorbed evil. Any house containing a sea bean was thought to be safe from fire. Richard Carew's *Survey of Cornwall* (1602) reports their use 'for women travailling in child-birth.' In Scotland and Norway, the beans often washed up on the western shores and they were frequently used as amulets to keep women safe in childbirth. The Scottish toxicologist Sir Robert Christison (1797–1882) recorded in 1866 that a Dr. Macdonald in Lochmaddy tried to get hold of a seed of *Guilandina bonduc* but was unsuccessful because, 'it is rare, and is so prized as a charm during childbirth that the midwives wear the seeds set in silver, for the women to hold in their hands while in labour; and a husband, who had two, refuses twenty shillings for one of them, saying he would not part with it for love nor money till his spouse be past childbearing.'

Peascod wooing was a familiar practice in England in medieval times. If an unmarried woman found a pea pod containing nine peas, she would place it above the door in the hope that the next man to walk through the doorway would become her husband. John Gay, an English poet and author of *The Beggar's Opera*, described this in his work *The Shepherd's Week* (1728):

'As peascods once I pluck'd, I chanc'd to see,
One that was closely fill'd with three times three,
Which when I cropp'd I safely home convey'd,
And o'er my door the spell in secret laid.'

Another medieval tradition is the baking of a Twelfth Night cake, a large fruit cake made to celebrate Epiphany, which was a much bigger feast-day than Christmas in those days. A dried bean and a dried pea would be baked into the cake and whoever found them became King and Queen of Twelfth Night. The King of the Bean, also known as the Lord of Misrule, would be expected to organise the evening's revelry. In France, the galette des rois is a round pastry made of two layers of puff pastry filled with almond paste. A fève (bean) was hidden within the galette and whoever found it in their slice was crowned the king or queen for the day. Nowadays the beans have been replaced by small ceramic charms but the finder still gets to wear a paper crown.

New Year's Eve dinners in Italy traditionally include a dish of lentils. Each lentil symbolizes a coin and eating them is meant to bring good fortune for the year ahead. The tradition dates back to ancient Rome, where giving a pouch of lentils symbolized a wish for a year filled with wealth and abundance. Brown or green lentils, such as lenticchie umbre from Umbria in central Italy, are used as they keep their shape while cooking.

In Japan, Setsubun is the day before the beginning of spring in the old Japanese calendar. On this day, soya beans are ritually scattered while chanting *oni-yarai* to expel any demons from the household.

Fig. 25. *Otafuku Throwing Black Beans to Chase Away the Demons on New Year's Eve* by Toshusai Sharaku (1795), The Art Institute of Chicago, reference no. 1934.197.

The bean-throwing is thought to have originated during the reign of Emperor Uda in the tenth century CE, when a monk on Mount Kurama supposedly escaped from a demon by blinding him with roasted beans. After spiritually purifying the house, it is customary to eat roasted soya beans, one for each year of your life and an extra one to bring good luck for the coming year.

Legumes in Literature

The Old Testament was likely written over a period of around 1000 years, from approximately 1400 to 400 BCE. References to legumes in the Hebrew Bible suggest that they were considered to be simple, humble foods. Esau sells his birthright to his younger brother Jacob for a 'mess of pottage' (Genesis 25:29–34). This was likely a meal of stewed lentils and the exchange is often interpreted to demonstrate the short-sightedness and misplaced priorities of the elder brother. During the siege of Jerusalem, Ezekiel was instructed to bake bread with mixed sprouted grains of wheat, barley, millet, spelt, beans and lentils (Ezekiel 4:9), a useful example of how to cope with limited supplies of flour in times of shortage. The Book of Daniel contains stories of miracles such as Daniel in the lions' den but also of an interesting dietary experiment. Daniel and his companions decline the meat and wine offered at Nebuchadnezzar's court and instead request that they are fed pulse vegetables for ten days: 'And at the end of ten days their countenances appeared fairer and fatter in flesh than all the young men that which did eat the portion of the king's meat' (Daniel 1:15).

In the ancient Greek satire *Plutus* by the playwright Aristophanes, first produced in 388 BCE, Chremulos comments that the gigolo has no further need for lentil soup since he has found wealth. *The Deipnosophistae*, written in Greek around 200 CE by Athenaeus of Naucratis in ancient Egypt, describes a series of banquets held at the house of the scholar Larensius; broad beans, grass peas, and lentils are included among the choice foods served to the guests. Shakespeare references pulses in several of his plays, including *Henry IV, Part 1*: 'Peas and beans are as dank here as a dog, and that is the next way to give poor jades the bots.' This is a comment by a carrier referring to the poor conditions at the Rochester inn, where the fleas were so numerous that they were biting the horses (jades). In *As You Like It*, Touchstone, while mocking romantic clichés, says, 'I remember the wooing of a peascod instead of her.' In *Twelfth Night*, Shakespeare uses 'peascod' as a metaphor for male maturity when Viola, dressed as the young man, is described by Maria as a squash that is not yet a peascod, implying the pod of a pea before the peas in it have developed as a metaphor for a boy before puberty.

Simplicius Simplicissimus, published in 1668 by the German author Johann Jakob Christoffel von Grimmelshausen (1621–1676), was one of the most widely read novels of its day. It tells the story of Simplicius a man raised by a hermit, who fights in the Thirty Years' War and his visits to both real and imagined countries. Simplicius goes on a pilgrimage to Einsiedeln in Switzerland with the soldier Ulrich Herzbruder. Herzbruder had been reluctant for the irreligious Simplicius to join him, but agreed on the condition they both walk with dried peas in their shoes so that every step would be painful, as he believed that a pilgrimage should be a journey of hardship. Simplicius agreed to the penance but by the time they reached Schaffhausen in northern Switzerland, the peas were hurting him so much that he boiled them before putting them back in his shoes. Peter Pindar (the pseudonym of the satirist Dr. John Wolcot (ca. 1738–1819)), used the story as the basis for his verse 'A True Story' in the late 1780s. Wolcot was said to have heard the tale from his grandmother, who referred to it when complaining about the irritating crumbs in her deathbed. Edith Nesbit's children's tale, *The Wouldbegoods* (1901), included a reference to the poem: '"People used to go pilgrimages to make themselves good." "With peas in their shoes," the Dentist said. "It's in a piece of poetry—only the man boiled his peas—which is quite unfair."' In 1807, *Simplicius Simplicissimus* (see figure 26) was printed as part of a series of humorous ballads, accompanied by an illustration by Thomas Rowlandson.

Grimmelshausen's tale was very well known and the idea of pea-boiling as a way of lessening a penance became part of popular culture. *Advice to Pilgrims*, a booklet written in 1830, suggested: 'Some pilgrims, it is true, have facilities for pea-boiling which others have not, and the peas which are put into the shoes of different persons are sometimes of different kinds, and require different degrees of boiling.' Professor Kathryn Hurlock of Manchester Metropolitan University pointed out that in reality, medieval pilgrimage placed little emphasis on the need for pilgrims to undertake an arduous walk unless they were performing an act of penance, and it was perfectly acceptable to ride.

The Danish author Hans Christian Andersen (1805–1875) was very well-read and it is likely he was familiar with Grimmelshausen's *Simplicius Simplicissimus*, but his fairy tale 'The Princess on the Pea' is thought to have been based on folktales Andersen had heard in his childhood. The story, in which a mysterious young woman is found to be a real princess because her skin is so delicate that she can feel a pea through twenty mattresses and twenty featherbeds, received mixed reviews with concerns that children may 'absorb the false idea that great ladies must always be so terribly thin-skinned.' The tale was first published with three others by Andersen in 1835.

A similar fairy tale, 'The Pea Test,' was included by the Brothers Grimm in 1843 in the fifth edition of their *Children's and Household Tales*. In his journal, Andersen complained that the

Fig. 26. *Pilgrims and the Peas* by Thomas Rowlandson after George Murgatroyd Woodward (1807) The Metropolitan Museum of Art, New York, object no. 59.533.986.

Grimms had stolen his story and noted that the German authors collected stories but never composed a tale themselves. The brothers Jacob Grimm (1785–1863) and Wilhelm Grimm (1786–1859) and French folklorists such as Charles Perrault (1628–1703) and Marie-Catherine, Countesse d'Aulnoy (1650–1705) generally chose to tell tales in the voice of those from whom they collected the stories. The Grimms certainly believed that many folktales were likely to be thousands of years old and so tales do not belong to an individual author, but to the people. In their retelling of the Bluebeard folk tale 'The Robber Bridegroom,' the resourceful heroine filled her pocket with peas and lentils and scattered them on her way through the forest to her suitor's house. After witnessing the murder of a young woman, she fled through the night helped by the peas and lentils which had sprouted and indicated the path in the moonlight.

Written in 1708, 'Art of Cookery' by William King (1663–1712) is a poem in the style of *Ars Poetica* (The Art of Poetry) by the Roman poet Horace from around 19 BCE. King satirizes the cookbooks of the era and includes some of the outlandish real recipes then circulating. He mocks cooks who create overly fancy dishes with whipped cream:

FIG. 27. The Princess and the Pea, illustrator Edmund Dulac.

'Pray what Relief
Will that be to a Saylor who wants Beef?
Who, lately, ship-wreckt, never can have Ease,
Till re-establish'd in his Pork and Pease.' Parents today of children with fussy eating habits may smile wryly at the child who 'makes great clutter,
Till he has Windows on his Bread and Butter:
He for repeated Supper-Meat will cry,
But won't tell Mammy what he'd have, or why.'

King advocated for the use of local seasonal ingredients and simple regional meals such as Leicestershire beans and bacon:

'The Farmer has brown Bread as fresh as Day,
And Butter fragrant as the Dew of May.
Cornwal Squab-Pye, and Devon White-Pot brings,
And Lei'ster Beans and Bacon, Food of Kings!'

Pulses have continued to provide inspiration for poets. London-born Ursula Askham Fanthorpe (1929–2009) published observant, often wry poems as UA Fanthorpe, including the delightful description of the kind of love, 'Which stores the WD40 and knows when to use it.' Her poem 'Men on Allotments' talked of 'drab solitary men' tending their plots while celebrating 'the unruly loveliness of beans.' Fanthorpe would probably have been pleased to hear that by 2020 more than 60 percent of London council allotments were occupied by women. 'The Bean Feast' by the Irish poet Seán Dunne (1956–1995) from his first collection, *Against the Storm* (1985) has a slightly melancholic feel to his exploration of the rich variety of beans stored in jars or soaking overnight in bowls beyond the pantry door. The much-loved American poet Mary Oliver (1935–2019) described walking between rows of beans, which 'like being lean,' in 'Beans' (2004), using the bean plant to explore themes of gratitude and goodness. The New Zealand author Katherine Mansfield (1888–1923) wrote a whimsical poem, 'An Escapade Undertaken by a Green Raspberry and a Kidney Bean' at the age of fifteen and in 'The Tiredness of Rosabel,' a short story about a young woman's fantasies of a more luxurious life written in 1908, Rosabel thought she would have sacrificed her soul for a good dinner—roast duck and green peas, chestnut stuffing, pudding with brandy sauce—something hot and strong and filling.

The classic children's novel *The Wind in the Willows* by Kenneth Grahame (1859–1932), first published in 1908, is widely acclaimed for its themes of friendship and love of nature. The food described, like the book's overall message, is straightforward: 'It was a simple but sustaining meal—bacon and broad beans, and a macaroni pudding; and when they had quite done, the Badger settled himself into an arm-chair.' Television programmes featuring fruits and vegetables, like role-modelling eating vegetables, seem to help increase consumption of these foods among school children. *The Poddington Peas* was a children's animated television series released in 1989 about a group of anthropomorphic peas, including Penela-Pea and policeman P.C. Pod whose dog was called Pup-Pea, which may be worth trialling with pea-averse infants. Definitely not for children was the 1991 American film *The Silence of the Lambs*, based on the 1988 novel by Thomas Harris. When a census taker tried to test him, the character Hannibal Lecter reported that, 'I ate his liver with some fava beans and a nice Chianti.' Christopher Hooton, writing in *The Independent* in 2015, pointed out that Lecter may have been making a medical joke and hinting that he had not been taking his medications. If he was on monoamine oxidase inhibitors, eating foods such as liver, beans and wine that are high in tyramine should be avoided.

Beanfeasts and Festivals

The word beanfeast was originally used for a meal or entertainment provided by an employer for their workplace employees. Beanfeasts may have included an excursion to the seaside or countryside, a trip to a country pub, or a picnic at a local beauty spot. On August 9, 1740 the weekly political newspaper *Common sense: or The Englishman's Journal* reported that, 'Last Week an eminent Brewer's Servants near Shoreditch, on their Return from a Bean-Feast at Camberwell, where probably they had made a little too free with their Malt Juice, resolv'd (as they call it) to take the Village of Walworth.' In 1805,

Fig. 28. *Pintura de Castas* by Miguel Cabrera (1763).

the *Sporting Magazine* reported, 'a Gentleman Taylor . . . gave a rich treat to his men, at his occasional country residence. It was called a Bean Feast; but . . . , the table literally groaned with bacon.' The poet John Betjeman (1906–1984), whose family ran a furniture business in Pentonville Road, remembered, 'beanfeasts with my father's firm' to 'Epping Forest glades.' By the Edwardian era, 'beanfeast' was often abbreviated to 'beano,' from which the British comic magazine *Beano*, first published in July 1938, got its name. The longest-running strip in the comic features Dennis the Menace and his dog, an 'Abyssinian wire-haired tripe hound' named Gnasher. Dennis is a badly behaved schoolboy who wages campaign of terror with his peashooter firmly aimed at Walter the Softy.

A peashooter is somewhat less lethal version of the blowpipe and they have been used with enthusiasm by small boys around the world for hundreds of years. The Mexican painter Miguel Cabrera (1695–1768) depicted the Casta family in 1763, showing the son shooting peas at his sister. In 1971, Mr. John Tyson, headmaster of the village school of Witcham near Ely in Cambridgeshire, caught some mischievous pupils shooting peas at their classmates. He confiscated their weapons but then came up with the idea of holding a Peashooting Championship alongside the annual Village Fete. Now known as the World Peashooting Championship, it has been held each July for over 50 years.

One of the oldest food festivals in the world, dating back over 700 years, is the Conwy Honey Fair in Wales, but there are many

Fig. 29. Sheet music for Hello! Old Bean, sung by Miss Olive Turner.

others. The famous Spanish La Tomatina, a tomato-throwing festival is held in late August in Buñol. Perhaps more esoterically the Räbechilbi turnip festival, held annually in Switzerland showcases artistically carved turnip lanterns paraded through the village of Richterswil. The Palouse region of the northwestern United States grows around a quarter of all the lentils raised in the United States and in 1989, the National Lentil Festival was started in Pullman, Washington to encourage tourism to the region and to promote the locally grown pulses. It features a parade, lots of music, and bowls of chilli lentils. The village of Peasenhall in Suffolk possibly derives its name from 'Pisenhalla' (a valley where peas grow) and there has been a settlement there since Roman times. Unsurprisingly, albeit intermittently, the village holds a Peasenhall Pea Festival to raise money for the maintenance of the village hall. Events have included Pea Shooting, the World Pea Podding Championships, the National Pea Eating competition, and a contest to create 'Leaning Towers of Peasa' using peas and cocktail sticks.

Legumes feature too in many of our idioms. To 'spill the beans' means to reveal a secret whilst someone who is 'full of beans' will be lively and energetic, or in some regions, full of nonsense or exaggerating. Something that is 'not worth a hill of beans' is worthless or insignificant, a term is popularized by a line of dialogue in the classic movie *Casablanca* (1942), in which Rick Blaine told Ilsa Lund during the film's climax, 'the problems of three little people don't amount to a hill of beans in this crazy world.' The phrase 'old bean' is sometimes used as a term of endearment particularly towards a man, with a suggestion of upper-class familiarity. The song *Hello! Old Bean*, with words by Jeffrey Vallis and music by Jan Hurst was published in 1919 and was sung by the composer and vocalist Olive Turner (1890–1954). The same greeting was used by Princess Anne when she spoke to her brother, King Charles III, after his coronation.

Chapter 4
GROWING AND PROCESSING

I will arise and go now, and go to Innisfree,
And a small cabin build there, of clay and wattles made;
Nine bean rows will I have there, a hive for the honey bee,
And live alone in the bee-loud glade.
William Butler Yeats, 'The Lake Isle of Innisfree' (1889)

Growing your own vegetables can be a particularly satisfying experience, even if you do not live in a bee-loud glade. Not only will your produce save you money on food bills, it ensures that the food you eat can be freshly-picked and full of vitamins, rather than added chemicals. It helps the environment too by reducing packaging and the food miles involved in transporting goods around the country. Working in a garden or an allotment is great exercise, helping to promote fitness, and just as importantly, being outdoors and in regular contact with nature can improve mental health and your quality of life. The American novelist Nathaniel Hawthorne (1804–1864) wrote in *Mosses from an Old Manse* (1846), 'It was one of the most bewitching sights in the world to observe a hill of beans thrusting aside the soil, or a rose of early peas just peeping forth sufficiently to trace a line of delicate green. Later in the season the humming-birds were attracted by the blossoms of a peculiar variety of bean; and they were a joy to me, those little spiritual visitants, for deigning to sip airy food out of my nectar-cups.'

Of course, there will be frustrations too. The weather will be too cold or too hot or the wind will blow your bean poles over. There will be no rain when you need it and too much when you don't. Sometimes you will think not of Yeats but of Edwin Muir's *Difficult Land*, with sun, rain and frost alike conspiring against you. And just when you think that perhaps you are going to have a good crop after all, the deer or the rabbits will move in and take the lot. However, peas and beans generally require little outlay or effort to grow and, so long as you are realistic in your expectations, a successful crop from your own garden will be extremely gratifying.

If you are new to gardening it is worth chatting to neighbours (or perhaps surreptitiously peering over some fences) to find out what grows well in your area. Local gardens open for charity may have vegetable gardens to inspire you or there could be a neighbourhood garden society that you can join. Getting to know enthusiasts who live nearby will enable you to exchange knowledge and perhaps to swap seeds and cuttings. Many commercial seed suppliers put far more seed than you really need in a packet, particularly when you are still at the experimenting stage, so it is worthwhile sharing the surplus and perhaps receiving something new that you had not considered trying in return.

Growing Your Own Legumes

If you do not already have a vegetable plot you will need to consider what space is available to you. You may have set your heart on an ornamental potager like the Renaissance potager at Villandry in France or have your name down on the waiting list for an allotment, but on a smaller scale you can easily grow a few beans in a bucket or experiment with peanuts in a grow bag. You should also consider how much time you have available. If you work long hours you may want to avoid crops that require regular watering such as runner beans. A sheltered, sunny spot is generally best for growing vegetables but they actually do not need a separate area. You could integrate a wigwam of climbing beans within an ornamental flower border or train some to scramble up a large shrub or an apple tree. If your garden consists of just a narrow bed against a fence then you can staple some netting against the fence to give peas and beans something to scramble up. Natural jute netting is available which, being biodegradable, means you can just compost it at the end of the season.

To give your plants the best start in life, prepare the soil by removing weeds and adding well-rotted compost or manure which will encourage worm activity and help to retain water, then rake the surface level. Raised beds can be easier to work than a flat site. Often thought of as a recent trend, Walahfrid Strabo (ca. 808–849) described creating oblong beds raised a little above the level ground and facing them with planks so the soil should not be washed away. Placed in the Benedictine Abbey of Reichenau at the age of eight, Strabo wrote his poem *Hortulus* in Latin hexameters. It is considered one of the earliest works of advice for gardeners. He suggested that whatever land you possess, whether barren with dead sand and gravel or rich, moist ground, your soil will not fail you so long as 'you do not let laziness clog your labour.' He spoke as the voice of experience—having wrestled with nettles, spread basketfuls of dung on infertile soil, and toiled with brimming buckets of water when the rain did not fall—and vividly described the joy that can be experienced by devoting time to a garden and waiting impatiently for seeds to germinate.

Actually, with peas and beans it can be surprising how quickly they germinate. They will often start to poke through the soil in only a few days making them ideal plants to grow if you are impatient or have children. The chunky seeds are easy for small hands to deal with. Planted in modular trays or individually in pots, paper cups, or the inner tubes of toilet rolls, peas and beans can be satisfying to watch on a sunny window sill. Starting seeds indoors keeps them safe from mice and the young plants away from slugs and snails. Peas are hardy plants so they can be sown outdoors early in the growing season and are reliable in most gardens. Broad beans are able to resist some frost and can be sown in the autumn in mild areas for a spring crop, although if sown too early they will be more prone to disease and to the effects of severe winter weather. The top growth may be hit if frost is severe but plants will usually send up new shoots from the base. Though beware that overwintering seed may prove irresistible to rodents. Seed for the main season crop can be planted in any mild spells after the winter solstice. Early maturing cultivars such as 'Luz de Otono' and 'De Monica' may also be sown in mid-summer for an early winter crop.

Fig. 30. Germinating beans on the kitchen windowsill.

Runner beans are tender plants that will be destroyed by frost. They will not thrive in very cold and exposed sites but will provide a generous crop in most areas. French beans usually need a warmer site but will produce bumper crops in good summers. Butter beans and lablab beans are also heat lovers. For early crops and in colder locations, sow seeds of most beans in a glasshouse, polytunnel, or on a windowsill in spring to provide a longer growing season. Seeds can be sown directly outdoors too, from late spring to mid-summer, after the soil has reached at least 10°C (50°F). If you do not happen to have a thermometer handy, the traditional gardener's method of checking the temperature was to drop your trousers and sit on the soil. If you can sit there comfortably, it is probably warm enough for the beans to grow. Lentils and chickpeas tend to prefer longer, warmer summers and need a warm, dry autumn to ripen but there is growing interest in developing new cultivars to suit local conditions in order to boost food security and sustainability. The Royal Horticultural Society (RHS) has been experimenting with these and other more unusual crops at their different garden sites across the United Kingdom.

Plants that start in a protected environment may need a transition period to get them used to the conditions outside. Hardening is the process of gradually letting young plants adapt to the sunlight, wind, and fluctuating temperatures outdoors. Start by putting plants outside for an hour or so one day, working up to 5 or 6 hours over a period of a week. Try to avoid putting them in full sun or windy situations while they acclimatise If you have a cold frame or glass cloche, this can be a useful halfway stage between the heated environment and outdoors. Alternatively, cover young plants with a layer of horticultural fleece until they are established, providing protection against many pests as well as the weather.

Climbing plants will obviously need something to climb. Climbing beans are often known as pole beans and they will happily twine around a pole, stout bamboo cane, or similar support. They are traditionally trained on bamboo wigwams, which are quick and easy to create by tying canes together at the top or using a ready-made cane joiner. Climbing peas tend to scramble around rather than reach for the skies and will also need some lateral support. This can be provided by stretching pea netting between supports or by using pea sticks which are the bushy twigs resulting from pruning trees and shrubs in winter. Robert Frost describes using his neighbour's birch prunings for this purpose in his poem 'Pea Brush' (1916). If you are artistic, the flexible stems of willow and dogwoods can be used to create beautiful and environmentally friendly obelisks and other supports.

Although many peas and beans will self-pollinate in the absence of insect pollinators, studies have demonstrated that pollination by bumblebees will increase the yield of most cultivars. You can encourage pollinators by providing some areas of long grass for bee nesting and planting a good variety of plants to provide pollen and nectar-rich flowers throughout the year. Make sure you have some late-winter/early-spring flowers such as winter honeysuckle, hellebores, crocus, and snowdrops so that queen bumblebees have a nectar source when they emerge from hibernation and can get a good start to the season. Avoid using insecticides, particularly immediately before or during crop flowering. Encourage natural predators such as wild birds, hedgehogs, frogs, and toads into the garden as they can be beneficial allies in the war against insect and rodent pests. Trees and shrubs will provide birds with shelter and cover from predators. Supply a variety of nest boxes to encourage breeding birds to use the garden as even small birds can consume large quantities of aphids and other pests when rearing a family. Providing water and supplementary feeding will help birds through hard winters. Having a small pond in the garden will also encourage frogs, toads, and slow worms, which are enthusiastic consumers of slugs and snails.

The second Viscount Townshend, Charles 'Turnip' Townshend (1674–1738), was a key driver of the British Agricultural Revolution in the early eighteenth century. He travelled extensively, particularly to the Netherlands where he saw first-hand the Dutch farmers' use of crop rotation and soil management techniques. He put this into practice on his lands at Raynham in Norfolk, integrating turnips and the leguminous plant clover into the farming cycle with barley and wheat. This became known as the Norfolk Four Course Rotation. Although this seemed revolutionary in Britain at the time, farmers have long recognized that suitable rotations such as alternating spring crops for livestock with cereals for human consumption make it easier to maintain productive soils. If crops from the same family are grown on a piece of land year after year there can be a build-up of soil-borne pests and diseases.

Crop rotation also helps to make efficient use of soil nutrients as different crops have different nutrient requirements. Alternating between deep-rooted and fibrous-rooted crops may help to improve soil structure. Including legumes in a rotation enables the nitrogen that they fix in the soil to be used for the next crop.

Although crop rotation started as an agricultural practice, changing the position of annual crops in the garden each year may be helpful. If using a four-year crop rotation, simply divide the vegetable garden into multiples of four. For example, in the first area plant tomatoes and other members of the same family such as aubergines and potatoes with root crops such as carrots and

First Plot	**Second Plot**
Year 1	*Year 1*
Tomato family and root crops	Brassicas
Year 2	*Year 2*
Onion family	Tomato family
Year 3	*Year 3*
Legumes	Onion family
Year 4	*Year 4*
Brassicas	Legumes
Third Plot	**Fourth Plot**
Year 1	*Year 1*
Legumes	Onion family
Year 2	*Year 2*
Brassicas	Legumes
Year 3	*Year 3*
Tomato family	Brassicas
Year 4	*Year 4*
Onion family	Tomato family

beetroot. Follow with members of the onion family and the next year, grow legumes such as peas and beans. Follow the legumes with brassicas such as cabbages and broccoli which have a high nitrogen requirement, before returning to the tomato family and root crops again. Growing tomatoes in a rotation after cabbage or sweetcorn has been found to reduce the incidence of bacterial wilt. Keeping to a strict rotation in a small garden can be impractical. To be completely effective the rotation would anyway require a much longer timescale than the usual three to four years as some diseases such as the disease of brassicas, club root, caused by the soil-borne slime mould *Plasmodiophora brassicae*, can remain in the soil for twenty years or more.

Sourcing Your Seed

The simplest and probably one of the cheapest ways to source pulse seeds is just to buy a bag of dried peas, beans, lentils, or chickpeas at the supermarket and sow a couple of handfuls before you cook the rest. Choose the whole pulse and not split peas, lentils, or dal. These have had the outer seed coat removed and are then split in half along the natural seam between the two seed leaves. This makes them easier to cook but they will not germinate. Some countries, such as New Zealand, require that certain imported edible seeds are heat-treated, which will make them impossible to germinate. Sourcing pulses that have been grown in your own area will give you the best chance of a successful crop yourself. If you are someone who does not like to leave things to chance, you will want to explore the range of cultivars available at a garden centre or specialist seed supplier.

When it comes to choosing varieties, you can look for those that have performed well in trials and received the RHS Award of Garden Merit (AGM), such as the broad beans 'Aquadulce Claudia' and 'Robin Hood' or the sugarsnap pea 'Sugar Lace.' Before the advent of hybrids all seeds were open-pollinated. Open-pollinated seeds rely on natural pollination from insects or the wind. Open-pollinated seeds which have been passed down from generation to generation are often called heritage or heirloom varieties. Many of these have interesting histories to them which add an extra dimension to the gardening experience. The climbing French bean 'Cherokee Trail of Tears' for example, commemorates the forced relocation in the 1830s of the Cherokee Nation from their ancestral lands in the southeastern United States to Indian Territory (present-day Oklahoma). The bean produces small black seeds that are usually dried for pulses. There are several organisations that try to preserve these heritage cultivars for future generations. In the United Kingdom, the charity Garden Organic maintains a Heritage Seed Library that holds more than 800 varieties of seeds. These include rare landrace varieties adapted to specific growing conditions, heirloom seed varieties, and many more recent cultivars that are no longer commercially available. Heritage varieties of vegetables are less likely to survive than fruit as they have shorter lives, therefore growing such plants and saving the seed yourself means that you are helping to preserve them.

F1 hybrid seeds are created by line-breeding two separate parent varieties which are then cross-pollinated. This process produces offspring that may exhibit superior traits such as uniformity, increased vigour, disease resistance, and improved yields. The seed will be more expensive to reflect the extra work involved in raising it. For a commercial grower, the uniformity and predictability of the crop

Fig. 31. Heritage seeds of the 'Yin Yang' beans.

may be worth the extra expense whereas a private grower may prefer their crop to ripen over an extended period rather than all at once. Peas and runner beans cannot be easily inbred and so these are usually only available as open-pollinated seed.

Some suppliers can provide seed that is pre-inoculated with symbiotic *Rhizobium* bacteria which help the plants to fix nitrogen from the soil. Many soils will already have these bacteria living there, especially if peas or beans have been grown previously, and these will naturally colonise the new plants. However, different legume species may require a specific species of rhizobia to form nodules and fix nitrogen so pre-treated seed may be useful. Once you have grown a crop in the soil, the bacteria will be present and you will not need to buy inoculated seed again. Using nitrogen-based fertilizers for legumes is usually counterproductive because the plants tend to stop nitrogen fixation when soil nitrogen levels are high.

Growing Peas

Peas are easy to grow. There are both climbing and bush cultivars. Climbing peas, such as the heritage cultivar 'Telephone,' were popular in the Victorian era but have fallen out of favour commercially because they are more difficult to harvest. They need some support but are useful plants for the home gardener as they continue to produce pods for many weeks and provide a generous supply of pea shoots—those tender, leafy tips and tendrils much favoured in salads, sandwiches, and stir-fries. Bush cultivars only grow to around knee-height. These produce all their pods in one flourish and then die back. Compact varieties, such as 'Half Pint' or 'Tom Thumb,' can even be grown in a tub or hanging basket. Sow peas outdoors or start them indoors in pots, modules, or old egg cartons to give them a good start and provide protection from pests. You can sow a succession of peas every couple of weeks from early spring until mid-summer to provide a continuous harvest over several months. Pick the pods regularly to ensure a long crop. Early varieties of peas such as 'Douce Provence' or 'Meteor' can be sown at the end of summer for an autumn harvest or towards the end of the year for an early crop the following year.

German immigrants living in Pennsylvania used to plant peas under the sign of Gemini (from May into June) hoping to get

FIG. 32. Vintage seed packet.

double pods to boost their harvest. Many modern cultivars have been selected for their productivity, yielding two pods per node instead of one without any astrological intervention. 'Kelvedon Wonder' is a reliable, early-maturing, climbing pea that mainly produces double pods of wrinkled peas. It was released in 1925 by the firm Hurst and Son who had trial grounds at Feering, near Kelvedon in Essex. Other tall peas include 'Alderman,' 'Radeo,' and 'Blauwschokker,' a heritage variety of shelling pea with striking purple flowers and deep-purple pods that can be eaten as mangetout when young or as mature peas. It often has nine peas per pod should you wish to try peascod wooing. 'Champion of England' is a traditional tall variety that Charles Darwin grew and mentioned in his book *The Variation of Animals and Plants Under Domestication* (1868). 'Lord Leicester' is a nineteenth-century variety that has been rescued by heritage vegetable enthusiasts and is appreciated for its plump, well-filled pods which are produced over a long season. As Mendel noted, garden peas produce either smooth or wrinkled peas. Smooth varieties tend to be hardier and so are better for early sowings while wrinkled varieties have a sweeter flavour. This is because wrinkled peas are deficient in the 'starch-branching enzyme' which reduces the peas ability to store starch, hence a higher sugar content.

The mangetout, or snow pea, type do not need to be shelled as the pods are sweet and tender, containing fewer tough fibres than standard peas. They are typically harvested before the peas have fully developed while the pod remains almost flat. As the name snow peas suggests, this type can withstand a certain amount of frost and snow and will begin producing in early spring once the snow has gone. 'Oregon Sugar Pod' is a tall growing mangetout type with really large broad flat pods. 'Jaune de Madras' was one of the yellow podded peas that Gregor Mendel grew when working on plant genetics. 'Golden Sweet' has purple flowers followed by rich lemon-yellow pods. With a name like 'Bijou' you would expect small, elegant pods but this cultivar has huge edible pods which are sweet and juicy.

Sugar snap peas, like snow peas, have edible pods but are instead rounded with crisp, thick pod walls rather than flat. A snap pea was known in Europe in the nineteenth century but the modern hybrids derive from a cross between a shelling pea and a snow pea. They are best harvested when young because if they are left too long, snap pea pods may need to be 'stringed' to remove the membranous string running along the top of the pod. 'Lusaka' is a productive cultivar that has been bred to be stringless. 'Sugar Magnolia' has magenta flowers and deep purple pods. It was named by Alan Kapuler of Peace Seeds in Oregon after the Grateful Dead song.

Marrowfat peas are allowed to mature longer in their pod than other varieties and are high in starch. Due to their larger size, marrowfat peas are often used for mushy peas and for canning. 'Maro' is the most widely available cultivar for gardeners. 'Rosakrone,' an heirloom from Sweden, has beautiful red and pink flowers held above the foliage. The peas can be eaten while immature as petit pois or left to mature and accumulate starch so they can be boiled and mashed as marrowfat peas. 'Akacia' is a really unusual pea cultivar, known as the parsley-leaved salad pea, which has a mutation that results in tiny leaves forming on the high-branched tendrils so that they look like bunches of parsley. This variety is grown for the pea shoots rather than the peas.

Peas may be prey to the pea moth, a grey-brown moth whose larvae feed within the pods, as well as aphids, pea and bean weevil, slugs, and snails. Mice, other rodents, and pigeons may eat newly-sown seeds. The long-tailed blue butterfly (*Lampides boeticus*) is one of the most common butterflies in the world, found from Europe to Australia. It is a migratory species and a few make their way to the UK each year, with climate change perhaps leading to them being seen more regularly. The caterpillars feed on plants in the legume family, including the narrow-leaved everlasting-pea (*Lathyrus sylvestris*). They also eat mangetout peas and so may occasionally be accidentally imported with a crop, but because the butterflies are so exquisite, they are best treated as an unexpected small joy, not a pest. Peas can also be prone to various fungal, viral, and bacterial diseases including powdery mildews, downy mildews, fusarium wilt, grey moulds, and pea leaf and pod spot. Fungal spores will overwinter on plant debris and spread through rain or watering so it is best to clean up the remains of any plants at the end of the season.

Growing Broad/Fava Beans

The field bean or fava/faba bean is grown mainly as a field crop. The familiar gardener's broad bean is the same species but tends to have fatter, longer pods and bigger seeds. Broad beans will grow in any reasonably sunny, sheltered site in rich, free-draining soil. Whether sowing direct or planting out, allow 20 cm (8″) between plants, with rows 60 cm (24″) apart. They need little maintenance, apart from watering in dry spells. Once the lowest set of flowers has formed small pods, pinching out the growing tip will encourage the plant to produce side-shoots, forming a bushier plant that will bear more flowers and pods. The young shoot tips can be used like spinach. Young immature pods can be picked when about the length of a standard wine cork for cooking and eating whole. Frequent picking once the pods form will encourage further cropping. For shelling, pick the pods when they are full but still relatively small, as these will be sweeter and more tender than mature beans.

Cultivars to try include 'Bowland Beauty' which has really long pods and 'Bunyard's Exhibition,' raised over 100 years ago. 'Dreadnought' is a heritage cultivar with seven or eight beans per pod. 'Aquadulce Claudia' is one of the best for autumn sowing. 'Karmazyn' and 'Red Epicure' have unusual red beans. Dwarf varieties such as the beautiful 'Red Bristow's,' 'The Sutton,' 'Oscar,' or 'Cole's Dwarf' can be grown successfully in containers or small plots. The early-maturing Italian cultivar 'Grano Violetto,' with its distinctive deep violet-purple beans, is another with beautiful flowers that is well worth growing in a cottage garden. Field beans, such as the cultivar 'Fuego,' can be grown as an alternative to broad beans. They can be more productive with many more pods to a plant, although have fewer, smaller beans per pod.

Dense colonies of black bean aphid (*Aphis fabae* agg.) may be found on the soft shoot tips, flower stems, and the underside of the younger leaves during spring and summer. These overwinter on shrubs and migrate to the beans in spring. They can cause stunted plant growth and a reduced yield. Light infestations can be ignored but pinch out any heavily affected shoot tips. Bruchid beetles can be a significant problem with agricultural crops of broad beans, particularly the broadbean weevil (*Bruchus rufimanus*) which is the largest species in the genus at 3.5–5 mm (1.5–2″). The adult beetle feeds on pollen while the larvae develop within the seed, leaving little round holes as they emerge. It is less prevalent in northerly regions. The most common fungal diseases of broad beans are broad bean chocolate spot caused by *Botrytis fabae* and broad bean rust by *Uromyces viciae-fabae*. Fungal diseases are more common in wet seasons. Destroy any infected plant material, and clear up any crop residues to prevent spores being carried over to the next season. Try to avoid damp, humid sites and space plants widely to maximise air flow. In some parts of the world the plant parasite *Orobanche crenata*, commonly known as bean broomrape, may grow on the fava bean. It is native to the Mediterranean basin in Europe and North Africa, the Arabian Peninsula, and Western Asia and has been introduced elsewhere. It has no chlorophyll and derives water and nutrients from the host plant. While plant parasites are interesting to see, infected bean plants will be less productive.

Growing French, Runner, and Lima Beans

French, runner, and lima beans are all from the genus *Phaseolus*, native to the Americas. The wild common bean *Phaseolus vulgaris* is the ancestor of an extensive range of edible beans, including the French and borlotti beans. Runner beans (*Phaseolus coccineus*) are also known as scarlet runners, due to the red flowers of most of the early introductions. Lima/butter beans (*Phaseolus lunatus*) will grow in similar conditions. All three species are sensitive to frosts so are usually grown as annuals. The seeds need warm conditions to germinate. They can be sown outdoors after the last frosts or under protection to give a longer growing season. Seedlings grow quickly and will benefit from planting in rich, moisture-retentive soil. If the soil is not suitable, they can be grown above a trench full of rotting organic material. If you want to grow in containers, use a large bucket or tub, ideally with a capacity of at least 18–20 litres (about 5 gallons). Three or four plants can be grown in a standard grow bag, although grow bags are not easy to keep consistently moist and it may be better to transfer to a large pot. Climbing beans will need a support system and may need some initial training. Once the plants reach the top of the supporting structure, pinch out the tips to encourage vigorous flowering and a heavy crop. Runner beans grow well in cool, wet climates and are productive in the usual English summers but the flowers do not always form pods well if the weather is hot and dry whereas French and lima beans will be better in those

Fig. 33. Lima beans, 'O Del Papa.'

conditions. Start to harvest the pods when they are young and tender. Frequent picking and an occasional feed with liquid fertiliser will encourage more beans to develop throughout the summer.

Recommended French beans include 'Cobra' which has pale violet flowers and summer-long crops of sweetly flavoured stringless pods. Growing beans with yellow or purple pods adds interest to the garden and makes it easier to spot the beans on the plants when it comes to harvesting. 'Blauhilde' has lovely purple pods and 'Orinoco' or 'Sunshine' are good for waxy, yellow pods. 'Boston,' 'Purple Teepee,' and 'Sprite' are productive dwarf cultivars. Borlotti beans are the best-known beans for drying. 'Lingua Di Fuoco' is a flat podded variety with spectacular-coloured green and red pods. This variety can be used for both edible pods and shelled dry beans. 'Lamon' has variegated beans with pinkish red splodges on a white background and is the classic cultivar for the traditional Venetian pasta e fagioli. The bean 'Fagiolo di Lamon,' which has Protected Geographical Indication (I.G.P.) status in Italy, is cultivated in the fertile Lamon plateau of Belluno in the Veneto region of Italy and comes in four forms which differ in shape and size. Seed is available outside of Italy but without the Italian sunshine and soil, you will get variable results. The striking black and white 'Yin Yang' beans, also called orca beans as they look like miniature killer whales, can be grown like French beans. This heirloom variety from Mexico can be used as a green bean or dried for future use. The plants are compact enough to be grown in large pots and are quite productive.

Reliable runner beans include 'Red Rum' named for the Irish champion thoroughbred horse, three times winner of the Grand National. It is a red flowered cultivar that sets well in hotter summers producing good crops of stringless, well-flavoured pods. 'Black Knight' has attractive rich red flowers and pods that develop a striking purple colour which looks good in an ornamental potager or cottage garden. Sadly, as with purple sprouting broccoli and purple asparagus, the purple colour leaches out during cooking. The red flowers of runner beans sometimes attract birds which will peck them off to get to the sweet nectar. If this is a problem in your garden you can try one of the newer varieties with pink or white flowers. These will usually be left alone. 'Sunset' has unusual peachy-pink flowers, followed by medium length green beans. 'White Lady' produces heavy crops of tasty stringless pods. 'Saint George' is an early, high yielding cultivar with bi-coloured red and white flowers. Dwarf cultivars like 'Hestia' and 'Pickwick' are ideal for container growing. Plant breeders have introduced hybrids of runner and French beans to develop cultivars which will set pods reliably in changing weather conditions. 'Moonlight,' introduced in 2011, produces attractive white flowers throughout the summer followed by a profusion of long, stringless pods that look and taste like a runner bean.

Lima/butter beans require plenty of sunshine and long, warm summers. Start them off on a bright, sunny windowsill or in a glasshouse. Seed is not widely available in the United Kingdom although you may be able to source the heritage variety 'Fagiolo di Spagna' which gives three to five beans per pod. They can be cooked like a French bean if picked when young. There is much more choice in the United States including bush varieties like 'Fordhook 242' or 'Henderson' which are ideal for container growing.

Most beans are easy to grow and generally trouble-free. If a late cold-snap is forecast after you have planted them out, cover your plants overnight with cloches or a layer of fleece. Seedlings and young plants are vulnerable to slugs and snails. Black aphids can sometimes colonise the shoot tips. Plants will tolerate a certain level of damage and if helpful predators such as ladybirds are around you can usually leave them to deal with infestations, otherwise just use your finger and thumb to squash colonies.

Growing Lablab Beans

The hyacinth or lablab bean is a beautiful climbing plant that is worth growing in your garden if only to appreciate its ornamental properties. The wild species is perennial but in gardens plants are usually grown as annuals. They will not tolerate frost and need a long growing season, so start them off indoors in early spring. The seedlings initially grow slowly, but once established plants can be vigorous, out-competing many weeds and will tolerate drought or shade. They can grow on a wide range of soils but do not like to be waterlogged. Originating in hot, dry climates, the plants are heat lovers so plant them outdoors in warmer areas or grow in a greenhouse or polytunnel. The thick stems can reach 6 m (20′) in length and can be trained against a wall or along a pergola. The pretty flowers can be pinkish, purple, or white and are self-pollinating. The pods are varying shades of green and purple. They are at their best when harvested at finger size: the pod walls are tender and the beans are small and soft. The beans have a prominent hilum where it was attached to the pod. The roots can be dug up and stored in a pot somewhere frost-free to overwinter, like a dahlia. Leaves, roots, flowers, pods, and beans are all edible, however the raw beans contain cyanogenic glycosides that release cyanide when broken down, so they must be boiled before consumption.

Lablab is a short-day plant. This means that it does not flower until the days become shorter than the nights, which occurs around September in the UK. A collaboration between scientists at Kew and Southampton University is working to create more commercial forms of lablab which crop earlier in the season. The cultivar 'Ruby Moon' is available in the United Kingdom and 'Koala,' an earlier maturing type with cream seeds is, perhaps unsurprisingly, sold in Australia. 'Highworth,' a black-seeded, purple-flowered cultivar was introduced to Australia from Southern India. In some parts of India, small, curved-podded forms called 'papri' or 'papapdi' are eaten much like green peas. Commercial growers may inoculate the soil with specific lablab rhizobia for the first year to maximise growth.

Growing Chickpeas

Chickpeas prefer a well-drained soil and plenty of sunshine. They are useful for poor, stony soils and are quite drought tolerant. You can sow them directly outdoors in the spring or start them off in modules to protect them from pigeons and rodents. Allow them to develop four or five true leaves before hardening them off and planting outside. Chickpeas are not as hardy as garden peas but will tolerate quite low temperatures, including light frosts. Plants are self-supporting although inclined to sprawl a bit. They have lovely feathery leaves and pretty flowers that are white or purple in colour so make attractive pot plants. The Italian variety 'Principe de Florence' is white seeded and popular for the Tuscan chickpea flatbread known as Cecina Toscana. In the southern regions of Puglia and Basilicata,

FIG. 34. Chickpea hummus.

a deep black seeded selection known as 'ceci neri' is grown. It is slightly nuttier in flavour than the common chickpea and makes a striking-looking hummus. 'Kala chana' is a small black variety of chickpea grown in India.

Chickpea pods are usually ready to start picking starting about 10 weeks after sowing. They only contain one to three chickpeas, but if you pick regularly the plants will be productive throughout the summer months. Pods are covered in fine hairs. A fine reddish exudate is produced on the leaves in hot weather containing malic acid which is found naturally in fruits such as apples. It can irritate the skin so wear gloves when you are harvesting. The chickpeas can be eaten green and have a pleasant nutty flavour. In long, hot summers they should be able to ripen so you can dry and save the chickpeas for winter use.

Growing Lentils

Most commercially grown lentils are raised in India or Canada as they need a warm, dry autumn to ripen. However, over the last few years farmers in Germany and the United Kingdom have grown successful crops and many gardeners have been experimenting with them on a small scale. Lentil growing may not be the best use of precious garden space but certainly has a curiosity value and in warm summers can provide a useful crop. Sow in early spring in modules with two to three lentils per module and plant outdoors once they have three or four true leaves. Alternatively, once the soil has warmed up, sow directly outdoors in rows 30 cm (12″) apart. Lentil plants have a sprawling habit, growing to around knee-height, with slender branched stems. The small flowers can be pale blue, white, or pink and are followed by pods usually containing just 2–3 lentils. Lentils can be time consuming to harvest but you can pull up the whole plants when they start to turn yellow and hang in a potting shed or garage to allow them to dry out before splitting open the pods over an old tea towel or sheet. Cultivars to try include 'Rosanna' and 'Flora' and the green Puy lentils from France.

Lentils are not usually prone to pests, but slugs and snails may well decimate seedlings and pigeons can take young growth and the pods. Although the plants can be productive, trials by Garden Organic members found that home gardeners generally considered them too tedious to harvest and the majority of members would not grow lentils again.

Growing Peanuts

The peanut is a fascinating plant to experiment with. It forms a bushy plant up to 50 cm (20″) tall and across with attractive, divided leaves. The cheerful orange or yellow flowers are held erect and once pollinated the stem elongates, pushing the pod into the ground, where the peanuts mature. This is why they are often known as groundnuts. There are two different plant types. The erect Spanish cultivars produce clusters of pods close to the main stem and often have three or four small seeds per pod. Runner cultivars produce pods along low-growing stems from tip to base, with usually two large seeds per pods.

Some suppliers sell individual peanut plants in the spring, although usually at a price far higher than the value of the crop you may harvest. It is simple enough to use the seed from a packet of monkey nuts (peanuts in their shell) from the supermarket, so long as they are reasonably fresh. Do not use the ones which are roasted in their shells as these will not germinate. You can buy the ones intended for wild bird food but do not eat these because even though they should have been tested for aflatoxins, they will not necessarily meet the standards set for those sold for human consumption. Remove the shell but leave the red seed coats intact and plant the peanuts in free-draining compost in a large pot or a prepared garden bed. Peanuts do better in warm conditions, so ideally plant them somewhere that gets at least eight hours of direct sunlight. If you have unreliable summers consider planting them in a polytunnel or greenhouse, or start them off inside in a protected environment for the best results. Dark-coloured pots are useful to help keep the roots warm and promote growth.

Peanut plants are self-pollinating. Once the flowers form, mound the soil around the base of the plant so the stems can push into the soil. Each plant can produce 30 or more pods, with two or more peanuts in each. Modern cultivars such as 'Justmore' produce 3–4 peanuts per pod. When the foliage begins to turn yellow, stop watering for a couple of weeks. To harvest the peanuts, pull the entire plant out of the ground to expose the pods, shake off the soil, then spread the pods out in a single layer in a dry place for two to three weeks.

Peanut plants are susceptible to several diseases that attack the foliage, especially leaf spot, rust, and net blotch. These are more common in moist, humid conditions. Aflatoxin contamination of the seed, caused by the soil-borne fungus *Aspergillus flavus* can cause illness if eaten. Aflatoxins are known to be carcinogenic. Discard any peanuts that appear shrivelled, discoloured, or mouldy.

Growing Asparagus Peas

The asparagus pea (*Lotus tetragonolobus*) is an attractive addition to a cottage garden border with small but intensely red flowers. They can be sown directly outdoors or started indoors in spring and planted outside after the last frosts. The plants may benefit from some support, such as pea sticks, to keep them off the ground. Alternatively, plant in a pot or hanging basket so that they cascade over the sides, allowing you to keep an eye out for the pods. The young pods ripen in mid-to-late summer after you have finished harvesting the real asparagus. Pick the pods before they get larger than about 2.5 cm (1″), otherwise they can be tough and unappetising. They are high in tannins and can be quite astringent if eaten raw, but boiled in plenty of water they make an unusual and palatable vegetable.

If you have left the pods to pass the point when they get tough, allow the peas to continue to ripen. The seeds thresh fairly easy from the pods once they are thoroughly dry. If roasted in a slow oven until they reach a dark, cinnamon-brown colour, they can be ground and used as a caffeine-free coffee substitute. Indeed, in her 1829 book *The Frugal Housewife: Dedicated to Those Who Are Not Ashamed of Economy*, the American writer and social reformer Lydia Maria Child, advocated for drinking a beverage made of roasted garden peas rather than expensive imported coffee.

Growing Soya Beans

In 2014 the Permaculture Association ran a trial to find out whether soya beans could be successfully grown by home gardeners in Britain. Unfortunately, it was not a success with the majority of the eighteen participants finding no germination of the seeds and at only one site were more than 50 g of beans harvested. The commercial firm SoyaUK suggests the crop is best grown on light land in the south of the country. However, starting with new soya and lupin varieties from plant breeders in Ukraine, they have been developing new cultivars which are easier to grow, more weather hardy, and easier to harvest. Early-setting cultivars such as 'Elena' and 'Siverka' produce clusters of flowers at the top of thick, self-supporting stems.

Fans of edamame beans, which are the immature soya beans in their pods, may well wish to experiment with growing their own as these can be difficult to source and expensive in the supermarket. Seed is becoming more widely available. Start the seed in pots or modules on a windowsill or in a greenhouse using a good quality compost. Germination takes up to two weeks. Plant outside after the risk of frosts has passed, leaving around 15 cm (6″) between plants. They will grow best in rich soil in a sunny position. Pick the pods regularly for use as edamame beans, when the seeds are plump but still tender. To dry for use as soya beans, allow the beans to mature then lift the whole plants and hang them upside down in an airy garage or greenhouse to dry. Shell the beans and store in a cool, dry place.

Growing Lupins

Most species of lupins, including the beautiful garden cultivars, have bitter seeds that contain a high concentration of toxic alkaloids including lupanine. For edible beans you need to select low-alkaloid 'sweet' cultivars. These, such as the white lupin *Lupinus albus* 'Dieta' or 'Haags Blue,' that is a selection of the narrow-leaved blue species *Lupinus angustifolius*, do not need any special treatment before cooking. *L. angustifolius* is the most widely-cultivated species and is grown primarily in Eastern Europe and Germany as it is more frost-resistant. Sweet lupins will readily cross with any bitter lupins growing in the neighbourhood, so any seed saved can in the next generation give rise to plants containing toxic alkaloids. Therefore, rather than saving your own seed it is safer to buy fresh seed each year.

Plant the seeds in spring in a sunny, sheltered spot in free-draining soil. Lupins are more tolerant than other pulses of sandy and acidic soils and can cope with lower temperatures than soya beans. Unfortunately, they are particularly attractive to slugs, so you may need a couple of Indian runner ducks to patrol the vegetable patch. The large and somewhat intimidating lupin aphid (*Macrosiphum albifrons*), native to North America but now widely distributed, can also be a problem, particularly in long hot dry spells. These greyish-green aphids form dense colonies on the stems below the flowers, causing plants to wilt and interfering with pod formation. Squash any you see, or if you are squeamish, dislodge them with a jet of water. Fortunately, garden birds such as wrens and blue tits tend not to be squeamish and will help to keep them under control.

Preserving Your Harvest: Freezing, Bottling, and Drying

One of the prime joys of growing your own vegetables is eating them fresh from the garden on the day they are picked. However, with many peas and beans the more you pick, the more they produce, so it is easy to find yourself with a glut. Green and runner beans as well as garden or mangetout peas all freeze well and cook easily from frozen. When the beans are young and tender, blanching them is unnecessary and risks them becoming soggy when you cook them later, but as the season progresses, it is worth blanching them before freezing. To blanch, first wash your beans, remove any strings, and slice into your preferred sizes. Add to a large pan of boiling water and cook for 2 minutes. Drain and cool them quickly by plunging them into a bowl of ice water. Once they have cooled, drain again and pat dry with a tea cloth, then they are ready for freezing. To prevent them sticking together in clumps you can flash-freeze them by spreading them in a single layer on a baking sheet until solid, then transfer them to bags or freezer-safe containers. Dry seed can also be frozen and this is a useful option if weevils are a problem.

Surplus French beans and runner beans can be submerged in a flavoured vinegar brine or used to make a range of pickles and chutneys which are perfect for simple suppers with some cheese and good bread. You can also bottle (or can) green beans but because these are a low-acid food and pose a risk of botulism, it is important to use a pressure canner, not a water bath canner. Layering young beans with fine table salt in an earthenware salt pot is a simple method of preservation and enables you to add more beans as you harvest them, rather than having to prepare all the beans in one day. When you decide to use them, first rinse them thoroughly in cold water and then soak for two hours to reduce the salt content.

Pulses grown for drying, such as borlotti, butter beans, and 'Yin Yang' beans, should be sown early to give them time to reach full maturity. Allow the pods to fully ripen and dry out on the plant. They will become brown, dry, and brittle and you should be able to hear the beans rattling inside the pods. To harvest for storage, cut the plants at the base and remove the pods to dry them further indoors. Shell the pulses and spread them on some newspaper or old sheeting somewhere dry in a well-ventilated space to ensure they are completely dry and hard. If there is any moisture left when storing, the beans will go bad. Once dry, store them in a clean, airtight container in a cool, dark place. Beans will store well in an airtight container for at least one year but if kept too long can be sometimes difficult to rehydrate. Studies have shown that pinto beans stored for up to 30 years were still considered acceptable for eating by a consumer taste panel. The archaeologist Mary Shepperson reported that she and a colleague ate some 6,400-year-old Ubaid lentils for a bet, noting 'they tasted mostly of dust, just like modern lentils.'

Sprouting Beans

Sprouted beans have been eaten historically in many Asian cultures and now are popular worldwide. The technique is thought to have originated in China. Sprouted mung and soya bean seeds were eaten on long sea expeditions, such as the seven treasure voyages to the 'West Oceans,' led by Zheng He between 1405 and 1433. They provided an alternative to fresh vegetables and along with stored citrus fruits, helped to prevent the sailors succumbing to scurvy. Experiments have shown that many species of pulses produce significant quantities of vitamin C up to five days following germination in both light and dark conditions. Sprouting beans also improves their digestibility by reducing the levels of anti-nutrients, such as phytates. Sprouting activates the enzyme phytase, which breaks down phytate, and may improve the bioavailability of minerals including iron, zinc, and calcium. Most sprouted pulses can be eaten raw or cooked

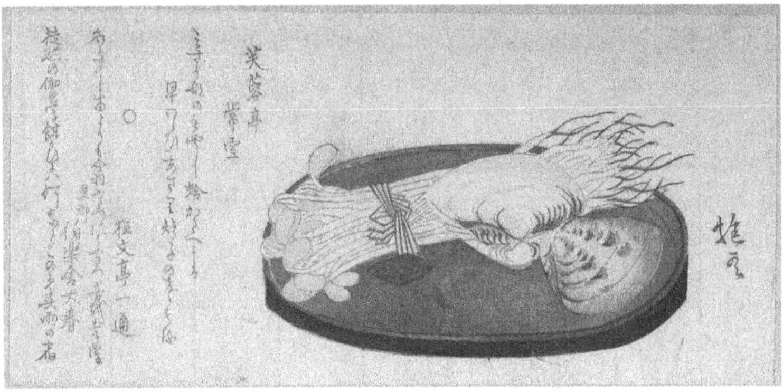

Fig. 35. Sprouted beans illustrated in *Malted Beans and Clams on a Red Tray* by Hōyū (Japanese) The Metropolitan Museum of Art, New York, object no. JP2268.

but some, such as kidney beans, should not be eaten raw as the naturally-present toxins are insufficiently broken down by sprouting.

Mung beans and soya bean remain the most commonly used but any legumes can be sprouted including alfalfa, chickpea, clover, fenugreek, lentil, and pea. Mung beans and green lentils tend to be the most reliable when you are starting out. Sprouted mung beans make a really good salad with chopped tomatoes, red onions, and some olive oil and lime juice. Green lentils have a particularly sweet, peppery flavour that is lovely in a salad or when eaten by the handful as a snack. Sprouting is very easy to do and does not require any specialised equipment. You can simply use a large jar with a piece of muslin, linen, or granny's old net curtains secured to the top.

- Day One: In the morning, place a handful of seeds in clean jar, cover them with just enough water that they are barely submerged, and place some muslin over the jar. After 12 hours, drain off the water, rinse the seeds, and top up with fresh water.
- Day Two: Continue rinsing and draining in the morning and the evening.
- Day Three: Many seeds will be now putting out roots (sprouting!) and they can be used while they are small and sweet or you can repeat the rinse and drain in the morning and evening.
- Day Four: The roots should now be a good size for use or you can continue to rinse and drain as before.
- Day Five: Seeds will be putting out their seed leaves. They will become tougher and lose their sweetness but will be fine for cooking in stir fries. Drain, rinse, and refrigerate if not using immediately.

The regular rinsing and draining is important as sprouted seeds can harbour pathogens such as *Listeria*, *Salmonella*, and *Escherichia coli*. Commercially-grown sprouts are grown in water heated to about 38°C (100.4°F), which is ideal for bacteria to flourish. They should be used promptly and health authorities suggest that raw bean sprouts should not be eaten by young children, the very old, or those with compromised immune systems.

Fermented Pulses

The process of fermentation has been used for food production and preservation for more than 10,000 years. Residue analyses of stone mortars show that cereal-based beer was brewed for Natufian ritual feasting using wheat or barley, oats, and legumes. Fermentation is not just used for the production of alcohol and pulses have been fermented in many different cultures. The use of fermented locust beans (*Parkia biglobosa*) in West Africa was documented as early as the fourteenth century and described by the eighteenth-century French botanist Michel Adanson, for whom the baobab genus *Adansonia* was named. Adanson learned the Wolof language to understand the specific terms that local peoples used to express particular properties of the native plants, although his opinions on social issues including slavery were censored by the French East India Company for whom he worked.

Fermented bean curd is a form of processed, preserved tofu made with soya beans, salt, rice wine, and sesame oil or vinegar. It has been made in China since at least the beginning of the seventeenth century and is commonly used as a condiment, combined into sauces, or consumed at breakfast to flavour rice, porridge, or congee. Miso is popular in Japanese cuisine for adding a deep, savoury, umami flavour to food. It is produced by fermenting rice, barley, or soya beans with salt and the mould kōjikin, generally known as koji (*Aspergillus sojae* or *A. oryzaea*). The resulting paste is used for sauces, pickles, and in miso soup. The traditional Japanese food natto is made from soya beans fermented with *Bacillus subtilis*. It is thought to have been first introduced to Japan from China during the Nara period (710–784 CE). The bacteria accelerates the breakdown of protein, releasing ammonia. The ammonia scent and mucous-like consistency of nattō make it something of an acquired taste.

Tempeh is a traditional soy product from Indonesia often used as a meat alternative. Whereas tofu is made from soya milk, tempeh uses the whole beans. It has a chewy texture and distinct taste. Tempeh is made by soaking soya beans overnight, removing the seed coats, and then boiling for 30 minutes. They are then drained, spread on a tray, and inoculated with spores of the fungus *Rhizopus oligosporus* from a piece of tempeh. The beans are then allowed to ferment for a day or two at room temperature. During fermentation, a white mould mycelium covers the beans and binds them together into a solid sheet. This is cut into smaller pieces for fresh use or is blanched, sun-dried, or frozen for future use.

Meju made from dried fermented soya beans serves as the basis of several Korean condiments and has its basis in ancient times. A Chinese historical text, *The Records of the Three Kingdoms* written in the third century CE, reported that 'Goguryeo people are good at brewing fermented soy beans.' To make meju the soya beans are washed, soaked overnight and then boiled or steamed for several hours. They are then drained and pounded in a mortar while still hot, and kneaded and shaped before drying in a cool shaded area until firm. Once hardened, the brick-shaped masses are tied with rice straws to the eaves of the house for air-drying, and fermentation with *Aspergillus oryzae* and/or *Bacillus subtilis*. The meju is then used in products such as doenjang (soya bean paste), ganjang (soy sauce), and gochujang (chili paste).

Plant-based alternatives to animal-derived food are increasingly popular but many people who will happily replace cows' milk with a plant-based alternative struggle to find an acceptable alternative to dairy cheese. Food technologists are now experimenting with mixing pea protein and sunflower oil. When fermented with lactic acid-producing bacteria, this develops a firm texture and produces some of the flavour compounds of dairy cheese.

Saving Your Own Seed

If Jack had not been in such a hurry to fell his beanstalk, he could have saved and sold the bean seed and would probably have made a huge commercial success. Saving your own seed is easy and is of course what people did for thousands of years before professional seed companies got involved. You can simply leave the last few pods on the plants when harvesting your crop and wait for them to dry out in late summer. However, if you want next year's crop to be the same variety as the one you have grown you will need to consider whether the plants are likely to cross-pollinate. Peas are nearly always self-pollinating, only occasionally crossing with other plants, so seed saved from any variety will generally produce a crop like that of the parent plants. Some plants such as broad beans and runner beans will readily cross with any other cultivars grown within a bee's flight and so are harder to keep true to form. Only grow one variety of these if you want to keep the seed pure, although even so you will get some variation if they cross with a neighbour's plant, as bees can travel up to 5 km (3 miles) in search of food. French beans are less likely to cross than runner beans and if you grow more than one variety in different parts of your garden it can be worth saving seed from each.

There is a great nostalgic appeal to growing heirloom varieties and for many gardeners, growing and saving seed from such plants is a way of connecting with their heritage or community. Of course, you can develop your own strains of favourite crops by watching and selecting for particular characteristics that appeal to you. Alternatively, you could actively breed your own plants by cross-pollinating two plants that show desirable traits and selecting the best offspring. By continually selecting and growing only the best plants you can create your own heirloom plants which could be passed down to future generations of your family or even introduced commercially.

To save pulse seeds, allow the pods to mature on the plant. Most cultivars will turn black or brown and brittle as the foliage dies back. When they are dry, collect the pods and break them open to release the seeds. Spread them out to thoroughly dry on a tray in a warm, well-ventilated place, removing any that look damaged or have weevil holes. Once they are sufficiently dry, your teeth should not leave a dent if you try to bite one. Store the seeds in paper bags or envelopes labelled with the variety and date, and place in an old biscuit tin or similar container somewhere cool, dry, and dark until time to sow in the spring. Make sure that they are out of the way of mice and other rodents who would be very glad to use your seeds as a winter food source. If weevils are a problem, you can seal the seed in a freezer bag and store in the freezer for a week after drying the beans to kill any insect eggs before they hatch. Allow the beans to come to room temperature when you take them out before opening the bag, otherwise they will absorb moisture from the air.

Most pulse seeds will remain viable for at least three years after harvest, so if you have spares remaining at the end of the season it is worth saving for subsequent years. Before buying new seeds, you can test the viability of old seeds by soaking a sample on moist kitchen paper to see if they germinate. If you trial ten seeds and find that only three or four germinate you can simply sow three times as many seeds as you normally would in a given area to yield a reliable crop.

Remember that seed saved from F1 hybrids will not come true to type, although they may still produce a useful crop. Some seed producers protect their investment by means of a patent or Plant Breeder's Right. This is a form of intellectual property that gives the producer exclusive control over the seed of a new variety seed for a period of typically 25 years. Growing seed saved from a protected cultivar would be subject to legal restraints. There have been concerns that some business corporations, in claiming that food crops are the intellectual property of the company, may harm the sustenance of farmers in the developing world. In 2008, the United States Patent and Trademark Office overturned a patent on a selection of yellow bean that was issued to a grower from Colorado in 1999. He claimed that he had developed a true-breeding strain of yellow bean that he called 'Enola' from a bean that he bought in a market in Mexico. The patent gave his company an exclusive monopoly and prohibited the importation or sale of any bean of the same yellow shade as the 'Enola' beans. Opponents of the patent argued that the bean had been eaten in Latin America for more than a century and maintained it was an issue of biopiracy. DNA fingerprinting undertaken in 2004 showed that the yellow 'Enola' bean was identical to a bean variety grown in Mexico.

Chapter 5
FINGER ON THE PULSE

There was an old person of Dean,
Who dined on one pea, and one bean;
For he said, 'More than that,
Would make me too fat,'
That cautious old person of Dean.

Edward Lear, *More Nonsense* (1872)

Nutritional Benefits of Legumes

Pulses are widely promoted as sustainable high-protein food sources with unique nutrient-rich profiles. Nutrients are those substances in foods that we need to keep us healthy. The English physician and chemist William Prout (1785–1850) was the first to propose the classification of the substances in foods into macronutrients: sugars, starches, oily bodies, and albumen. These would later become known as carbohydrates, fats, and proteins. Justus von Liebig (1803–1873), a German scientist, built on Prout's work and identified the nitrogen, phosphorus, and potassium in soils as essential to plant growth. It was in the early twentieth century that workers, notably the Polish biochemist Casimir Funk (1884–1967), looking at deficiency diseases—such as beri-beri, scurvy, and rickets—were able to identify the micronutrients called vitamins (from *vita* for life and *amines*, nitrogen-containing compounds).

Peas, beans, and other members of the legume family are undoubtedly valuable sources of protein. Dry pulses typically contain 21–25% protein which is almost double that found in cereal grains. All proteins are made up of amino acids, of which 21 are common to all life forms. Humans can synthesise all but nine of these. These nine—histidine, isoleucine, leucine, lysine, methionine, phenylalanine, threonine, tryptophan, and valine—are known as essential amino acids and they have to be provided by our diet for healthy bodily functions. A food source is said to be a complete protein if it contains an adequate proportion of each of the nine essential amino acids. Animal proteins, including meat, poultry, fish, eggs and dairy foods, are all complete proteins. All plant sources of protein also contain all the essential amino acids; however, most are low in certain amino acids. Cereal grains tend to be limited in lysine. The limiting amino acid for most pulses is the sulphur-containing amino acid methionine. In the context of a normal, varied diet, this is not important and by combining cereals with pulses in the diet the body can get all the essential amino acids it needs.

Soya is sometimes said to be a complete protein but, although it does have a higher methionine content than most other legumes, there is not really a huge difference. Soya beans have a Digestible Indispensable Amino Acid Score (DIAAS) of around 100, compared with peas which have a DIAAS of 80. Hence 50 g of pea protein gives you the same amount of the limiting essential amino acid as would 40 g of soy protein. Introduced in 2013 by the Food and Agriculture Organization, the DIAAS allows the assessment of a protein's quality based on the true biological digestibility of its amino acids and is considered to be the most accurate and reliable measure of protein quality for human nutrition. Scores for cereal grains show a wide range, with buckwheat having a relatively high score of 68, white rice 37, and whole wheat 20. Perhaps surprisingly, potato protein is even better than that of pulses, with a DIAAS around 125, that is similar to proteins from animal sources. Pulse proteins—unlike those of the cereals wheat, rye, and barley—do not contain the gluten group of proteins, so they are suitable for people who have coeliac disease or are otherwise intolerant of gluten.

In addition to protein, pulses are good sources of carbohydrates. Carbohydrates are food components containing carbon, hydrogen, and oxygen and include simple sugars, starches, and indigestible polysaccharides which are the main components of dietary fibre. Carbohydrates are the preferred energy source for the brain and nervous system. The fibre in pulses promotes a healthy digestive system and can help in managing blood sugar and cholesterol levels. The glycaemic index of a carbohydrate-containing food is an indication of how quickly the carbohydrates will break down and release glucose into the bloodstream. Pulses have a lower glycaemic index than many other foods which is attributed to their higher contents of indigestible carbohydrates such as dietary fibres and resistant/indigestible starches. These can increase satiety from a meal, making you feel full for a longer period of time.

Legumes are rich sources of both soluble and insoluble fibre, which together are valuable in preventing constipation by increasing stool bulk and promoting regular bowel movements. *The Book of Sent Soví*, composed around the middle of the fourteenth century, is a collection of recipes written in Catalan by an unknown author. In the chapter on legumes the writer observes, 'As during Lent one must often eat food that causes obstructions, such as fish and dishes eaten with a spoon, it will be a profitable thing for conserving one's health if one takes a bit of puree made with chickpeas or peas at the beginning of the meal.' It is unclear why the writer thought dishes eaten with a spoon would cause obstruction, but the bit of chickpea or pea puree should certainly help prevent that, particularly if taken with a glass of water.

Pulses are typically low in fats, around 2–3% of the seed mass. Some species such as chickpeas may have 6% or more fat content. Dried soya beans are around 20% fat and peanuts are relatively high in fat, containing around 50% total fat by weight in their raw state. This is why peanuts and soya are often classified as oilseeds, with a large portion of their harvest being used to produce oils. The majority of this fat consists of healthy monounsaturated and polyunsaturated fats, although some saturated fat is also present.

Other nutrients are also found in legumes, including iron and calcium. The gross calcium content has been found to range from around 30–300 mg per 100 g cooked product. Some brands of tofu can have a particularly high calcium content due to the addition of calcium salts during processing. It is important to consider not just the actual calcium content but how well that can be absorbed by the body. Studies have shown low bioaccessibility of calcium in tofu and many plant-based beverages despite having high calcium contents. The bioaccessibility was lowest for tofu (4%) and highest for peas (47%). Kidney beans and black chickpeas have moderate calcium bioaccessibility which combined with their high calcium density, means they can be considered as reasonable sources. Unfortunately, when both bioaccessibility and recommended serving portions are considered, few plant-based sources of calcium are as useful as dairy milk. Kale, finger millet (*Eleusine coracana*), and fortified white bread are good sources. Chickpeas, kidney beans, and peas are considered moderate sources of calcium, with 1.5–3 average servings being equivalent to the calcium found one serving of skimmed milk.

Iron in food exists in two forms: haem and non-haem. The haem iron found in meat is the most easily absorbed iron source by the body. Non-haem iron is found in vegetables, including pulses and grains and is less easily absorbed by the body. Eggs contain both haem and non-haem iron and their iron has limited bioavailability. Although beans, peas, and lentils can look to be excellent sources of iron on paper, some of their anti-nutritional factors, such as phytate (inositol hexaphosphate), can bind with the iron and other minerals including calcium, magnesium, and zinc to make them less available for the body. This reduced bioavailability explains the higher proportion of vegetarians (compared to non-vegetarians) who have iron deficiency anaemia. This is especially true for premenopausal vegetarian women. Vitamin C has been shown to increase the absorption of iron from the gut; however, it is not clear whether this will have a significant impact on actual iron status. Iron bioavailability varies between different cultivars of beans so eating a variety rather than just one kind may be beneficial.

Hazards

According to the government Office for National Statistics based on deaths registered in England and Wales from 2018–2022, an average of 219 people die each year as a result of choking on foods. The biggest cause is food which has not been chopped up correctly. The elderly and small children are more vulnerable to the dangers of choking and are typically more prone to accidentally ingesting or inhaling something inappropriate. Children are not able to fully master the chewing/swallowing technique until they are between four and six years old. Any food served to children should be cut into suitable-sized pieces. They should sit still while eating rather than running around and must be supervised. There are videos available online by organisations such as the National Health Service and the Child Accident Prevention Trust to help parents and anyone sometimes left with sole charge of a child distinguish between gagging and choking and to know what to do if needed.

Whole peas and beans can, like nuts, be a choking hazard and in Japan a 4-year-old boy died after choking on roasted beans at a traditional setsubun event in a childcare centre in Shimane Prefecture. In response, the Consumer Affairs Agency there published new instructions cautioning against allowing children five years or younger to eat whole beans or nuts. Most well-cooked pulses, however, are softer than nuts and can be easily squashed between a finger and thumb before giving to infants or they may be served safely by mashing them with other foods rather than serving in their whole form.

Gone with the Wind

First produced at the Lenaea festival of 422 BCE, *The Wasps* is a comedy written by the Greek playwright Aristophanes. In this play, the young Athenian Bdelycleon offers Philocleon a snack of lentils. Philocleon eats too much and develops a stomach ache, which makes his eyes water and is mistaken for tears of sympathy. Millennia later, many people will have sympathy with Philocleon as peas, beans, and lentils are notorious for causing abdominal pain, bloating and flatulence. The English botanist and herbalist Nicholas Culpeper (1616–1654) noted that 'chick-pease or cicers' are less 'windy' than peas and more nourishing. A century later the scientist and diplomat Benjamin Franklin (1706–1790), one of the Founding Fathers of the United States, wrote his fatuous *A Letter to a Royal Academy about Farting* (1781). His suggestion that scientific research should be undertaken to develop a drug that could be mixed with foods to render flatulence 'not only inoffensive, but agreeable as Perfumes' was not taken up.

Plant-based foods contain many non-digestible fibres which survive the acidic conditions of the stomach and pass through the gut to the colon where they are fermented by the beneficial bacteria naturally present there. Pulses contain lots of fibre including raffinose-type oligosaccharides which are also found in vegetables such as cabbage and broccoli. These are sometimes referred to as 'prebiotics.' They promote the growth of the beneficial microflora in the gut and are thought to play an important role in our overall physical health. However, those beneficial bacteria create gas during the fermentation process which can result in discomfort and embarrassing flatulence in susceptible people. A randomized crossover trial during which healthy adults were asked to eat either half a cup of peas or beans, or an equal quantity of carrots each day for 8–12 weeks, found that initially half the people reported increased intestinal wind while eating the pulses. However, after 8 weeks this had reverted to normal levels, suggesting that regular consumption of peas and beans may reduce the symptoms of bloating and abdominal discomfort.

For those people prone to unpleasant side effects when eating pulses, it may help to introduce them slowly. Start by eating just one to two tablespoons of beans per day and gradually increase to a half cup portion. This gives your gut bacteria time to adjust to the increased fibre available. Soak dried pulses for at least four hours and preferably overnight and discard the soaking water, then rinse thoroughly before cooking to reduce levels of soluble oligosaccharides. Canned beans should also be rinsed before use. Do not use the water to make aquafaba if you have a sensitive gut. Unfortunately, as the American food historian Ken Albala reports in his book *Beans:*

A History (2007), some people never fully develop the ability to eat beans without bloating.

Kombu, a type of kelp seaweed from the genus *Laminaria* is widely used in Japanese cooking. It contains alpha and beta-galactosidase enzymes which are reported to break down the raffinose carbohydrates in pulses making them easier to cook and to digest. Eaten with the pulses, it brings an umami flavour to the dish. The enzyme alpha-galactosidase is also available as a dietary supplement. A small double-blind crossover study showed that it reduced episodes of flatulence five hours after a test meal of meatless bean chilli; though there were no differences found in the extent of bloating or pain following the meal, but it may be worth trialling if other measures do not help. Certain herbs are sometimes promoted to break down gas-producing fermentable fibres. Epazote (*Dysphania ambrosioides*) is commonly used in Mexican cuisine, but care must be taken as the essential oils in the plant can themselves cause severe gastroenteritis with pain, vomiting, and diarrhoea if eaten to excess. Increasing concerns about the safety of herbal drugs, including cases of serious kidney damage, means that suppliers must apply for a traditional herbal registration (THR) before they can market a traditional herbal medicinal product in many countries. Because food supplements are generally regulated as foods rather than medicines, great care must be taken before use.

Plant Toxicity

The Scottish toxicologist Sir Robert Christison (1797–1882), known for his research on kidney disease and, less commendably, for his extreme opposition to women doctors, had an intense interest in scientific investigation and frequently experimented on himself. He was intrigued by the esere bean (*Physostigma venenosum*), endemic to tropical Africa, that was the subject of a paper presented to the Ethnological Society in 1846 by William Freeman Daniell, an English physician and botanist. Daniell came across the bean during his travels in Old Calabar, in what is now Nigeria, and reported that a decoction of the bean was used by the Efik people to determine whether individuals were innocent or guilty of serious misdemeanours. The prisoner was made to drink the liquid. If they vomited and recovered, they were declared innocent and set free, but death was considered to be proof of guilt. Missionaries in Calabar estimated that the seed caused some 120 deaths annually. Christison swallowed one quarter of a bean to see what effect it would have and experienced 'a peculiar indescribable torpidity of the whole frame' and twitching of the voluntary muscles. He saved himself by drinking his soapy shaving water to make himself vomit and got his son to call in a colleague to provide medical assistance.

Producing seed is an energy-intensive process for a plant, requiring significant resources to accumulate and store the nutrients for the seed's embryo and its initial growth upon germination. Seeds of course are attractive to animals due to their stored nutrients, and some animals such as birds and rodents will eat a large proportion of a plant's seeds while inadvertently providing an invaluable service in terms of long-range seed dispersal. However, many insects such as bean weevils will eat the seeds without providing any compensating benefit for the plant. Pulses therefore have evolved forms of chemical warfare against weevils and other pests, accumulating substances that are toxic to insects including lectins, saponins, and trypsin inhibitors. Many people confuse the word natural with benign. Plant toxins are perfectly natural but can be extremely harmful. Strychnine and cyanide, for example, are naturally present in plants and seeds. Many species in the genus *Gastrolobium* in the pea family are known as poison bushes because they produce fluoroacetate, which is highly toxic to domestic grazing animals. Birds and mammals including humans will be affected by many plant toxins, but reactions are not usually fatal. Saponins and lectins are usually water soluble, so soaking the seed followed by thorough cooking will degrade many of the toxins and make most pulses perfectly edible.

One of the most well-known of the natural toxins in beans is phytohemagglutinin. This consists of two closely related lectins called leucoagglutinin (PHA-L) and PHA-E. These are sugar-binding proteins which cause the blood cells to clump together. Phytohemagglutinin is found in many types of beans, but red kidney beans typically contain three times the level found in white beans and ten times that found in broad beans. Poisoning causes extreme nausea, vomiting, and diarrhoea, usually occurring within one to three hours of eating improperly prepared beans. Symptoms can result from as few as four or five red kidney beans. Phytohemagglutinin can be deactivated by cooking the beans vigorously for ten minutes in boiling water. After this initial boil, you can then continue to cook the beans at a lower temperature until tender, but the first boil is important as insufficient cooking, such as would occur in a slow cooker, will not deactivate the toxin. High-temperature pressure cookers will be effective and commercial canned beans are safe to eat without further cooking. Food prepared at high altitudes where the boiling point is reduced, may still be problematic, so do not take dried kidney beans with you on a camping trip to the mountains. Different cultivars of the same species of bean may have significantly varying levels of the phytohemagglutinin toxin, so all beans should be cooked properly before consumption.

The grass pea (*Lathyrus sativus*) was one of the first crops to be cultivated and archaeologists have found seeds in excavations from India and Turkey dating back to 8000 BCE. It is easy to grow, being resilient to both drought and flooding, palatable, and high in protein, so would seem to be a perfect crop. However, grass pea contains a neurotoxin known as beta-L-oxalyl-2,3-diaminopropionic acid (β-L-ODAP). Certain levels can be tolerated by the body but if grass pea is used as a major part of the diet in times of famine and scarcity, it can cause a neurodegenerative disorder called neurolathyrism which results in irreversible paralysis. This is most common in India, Pakistan, Bangladesh, and Ethiopia. The grass pea has been thought of as an 'insurance crop' in Europe as it produces reliable yields when all other crops fail. Grass pea feasts and festivals are still held in southern Europe, particularly in Italy and Spain. Outbreaks of neurolathyrism have historically occurred after famines in France, Spain, and Germany. The influential Spanish artist Francisco Goya (1746–1828) produced an etching *Gracias á la almorta* (Thanks to the Grass Pea; see figure 36) as part of his disturbing series *The Disasters of War* (1863). It depicts a woman who is paralysed by neurolathyrism, surrounded by starving people waiting for food during Napoleon's siege of Madrid. Grass-pea products were banned for

FIG. 36. *Gracias á la almorta* by Francisco Goya (1863).

sale for human consumption in Spain from 1967 to 2018 due to their toxicity. Researchers are trying to breed cultivars with reduced levels of the toxin using cultivars from western Asia. Soaking the peas prior to cooking with fresh water reduces the risk.

Osteolathyrism is a type of lathyrism that affects the connective tissues. It results from eating sweet pea seeds (*Lathyrus odoratus*). The word 'sweet' in sweet peas refers to the fragrance and not the taste as the seeds are inedible. They contain a different toxin (β-aminopropionitrile) which affects the linking of collagen, a protein of connective tissues. Angiolathyrism, which can result from grass pea consumption, is similar to osteolathyrism in its effects on connective tissue but is instead affecting the blood vessels (rather than bones).

Some toxins are produced not by the plant themselves but by fungi associated with the plants. The lupin species *Lupinus albus* is widely used in Australia in animal feeds but some lupin cultivars are susceptible to the fungus *Diaporthe toxica* which can cause a disease known as lupinosis in sheep. Plant toxins can sometimes actually be useful. The gum arabic tree (*Vachellia nilotica*, more commonly known as *Acacia nilotica*) native to Africa, the Middle East, and the Indian subcontinent has been found to be a powerful molluscicide. The fruits are used in ponds in Sudan to kill the snail species which carry schistosomiasis (bilharzia), without affecting fish in the water.

Favism

Favism is a genetic disease caused by a deficiency of the enzyme glucose-6-phosphate dehydrogenase (G6PD), which protects red blood cells from damage. Affected people are born with the condition and it stays with them for life. Damage of the red cells can occur when exposed to certain chemicals present in fava/broad beans, some drugs such as primaquine which is used in treating malaria, some industrial chemicals, and alcohol. This can cause haemolytic anaemia, a condition which happens when red blood cells are destroyed faster than the bone marrow can replace them. The first reference to favism appeared in an article published in Portugal by Mira Franco in 1843 which reported on the occurrence of jaundice after eating fava beans.

All those with favism are deficient in the G6PD enzyme, however not all G6PD-deficient individuals will develop haemolysis after eating fava beans. The term favism refers to an acute haemolytic episode in G6PD-deficient individuals that occurs after eating the beans, their pods, and potentially, their leaves. Indeed, some individuals are reported to be so sensitive that inhalation of the bean pollen may trigger an attack, the mechanism of which is not well understood. There have been a small number of reports of exclusively breast-fed infants who developed symptoms when their mothers ate fava beans. The glycoalkaloids vicine and convicine are the problem constituents in the beans. These are naturally occurring bitter compounds which act as a natural defence mechanism to protect the plant against pest and fungal attacks. The toxins are found throughout the plant but with the highest concentrations in the seeds.

G6PD deficiency can occur in people of all races and ethnic backgrounds and is believed to affect more than 400 million people worldwide. It is more common in the Mediterranean region,

Sub-Saharan Africa, the Middle East, Southeast Asia, and South America. In these regions, some 5–30% of the population is G6PD-deficient. Despite this high prevalence, the vast majority of people remain without symptoms throughout their lives. A severe form of the disease occurs more often in Mediterranean populations. The severity of haemolytic episodes can vary in the same person. The most frequent signs are jaundice (yellow colouration of the skin and whites of the eyes), black or red urine, back pain, fever, and generally feeling unwell. Babies with G6PD deficiency are sometimes more severely jaundiced than other babies and can require treatment to reduce the jaundice.

Haemolytic anaemia typically occurs 2–4 days after exposure to a trigger and in most cases, resolves itself once exposure stops. It can take about a week for the haemoglobin levels to improve and full recovery can take 3–6 weeks. Sufferers of favism are advised to avoid broad beans for life. Mature seeds are more likely to induce a crisis than immature ones and raw seeds will have higher levels than boiled or canned ones. Low vicine-convicine fava beans have been bred in recent years and are considered safe for consumption by G6PD-deficient individuals. However, some individuals seem to be more sensitive to trace amounts of the glycoalkaloids than others, reacting even to trace cross-contaminations in other foods. A study at the King Faisal Specialist Hospital in Saudi Arabia followed up with individuals who had experienced an episode of favism and found that among patients who had resumed eating fava bean for various reasons, the recurrence of symptoms was uncommon. The researchers suggested that an infectious agent such as a virus may play a role in the development of favism.

In 1913, the Swedish biochemist Markus Guggenheim found that the seedlings, pods, and beans of broad beans are rich in levodopa (L-Dopa). This can be converted in the body into dopamine, a neurotransmitter and hormone that plays a crucial role in brain activity and human mood and has a role in regulating heart rate and kidney function. In the late 1960s, L-Dopa was given to Parkinson's patients with encouraging results and it was used by the British neurologist Oliver Sacks to treat patients with encephalitis lethargica at the Beth Abraham hospital in the Bronx in New York State, as described in his book *Awakenings* (1973). This has led to suggestions that broad beans fed to Parkinson's disease sufferers could lead to a significant improvement in symptoms. However, a 2019 review in the open access journal *Parkinson's Disease* looking at broad beans and several other beans found no data on long-term efficacy or side effects of bean therapy was available and so expressed reservations about the use of beans as a 'natural' therapy.

Legume Allergy

A food allergy is an immune response to the proteins in a specific food, which the body mistakenly identifies as harmful. This can stimulate the production of antibodies called Immunoglobulin E (IgE) which are designed to target those particular proteins. These antibodies attach themselves to specialised cells called mast cells and basophils which are concentrated in areas of the body associated with the external environment such as the skin, nose, eyes, lungs, and digestive tract. When the proteins are encountered, the IgE antibodies are triggered to release chemicals such as histamine into the surrounding tissues. This can dilate blood vessels, increase mucus production, and cause inflammation, resulting in symptoms such as stomach pain or vomiting, runny nose, sneezing, itchy eyes, wheezing, and raised rashes called urticaria or hives. Reactions that involve the airway, breathing, and circulation are classified as anaphylaxis and can potentially be life-threatening. In extreme cases there can be a dramatic fall in blood pressure and the person can collapse. Anaphylaxis is a medical emergency: adrenaline should be given without delay and an ambulance called urgently with anaphylaxis as the reason.

Non-IgE mediated allergies are immune reactions that do not involve the IgE antibodies and tend to cause delayed symptoms occurring hours after ingestion of the allergen. Symptoms can include flares in eczema, vomiting, or diarrhoea and are usually milder, although conditions like Food Protein-Induced Enterocolitis Syndrome (FPIES) can be severe. This is a very rare form of food allergy and occurs mainly in infants, causing profuse vomiting and diarrhoea, which can lead to dehydration, lethargy, and sometimes shock, and may require emergency intravenous fluids for acute episodes. Non-IgE reactions to legumes appear to be uncommon, although soya protein does cause problems in some individuals with symptoms usually involving the digestive system. There are no reliable skin or blood tests to diagnose non-IgE mediated allergy, although there are unfortunately many people happy to make money by promoting unsubstantiated tests. It is important that food allergies are properly diagnosed by a healthcare professional.

The most widely recognised of legume allergies is to peanuts. Peanuts contain 32 different proteins of which 18 have been identified as potential allergens, with Ara h 1, Ara h 2, Ara h 3, and Ara h 6 considered major peanut allergens. Many of these proteins are seed-storage proteins which are designed to act as a food reserve for germinating seedlings before they begin to photosynthesize. They may also play a role in defence against plant pathogens. Most of the seed storage proteins of legumes are globulins which are insoluble in water and are able to resist heat, protein-splitting enzymes, and chemical denaturation. Many people with a milk or egg allergy are able to tolerate those foods in baked form as the proteins can be broken down by heat. However, the seed storage proteins present in legumes tend to be more resistant to heat. The processing of peanuts with dry methods, such as microwaving, roasting, and frying at high temperatures is thought to actually increase their allergenicity particularly of the Ara h 1 and Ara h 2 proteins, whereas cooking with wet methods, such as boiling and high-pressure steaming/autoclaving may decrease their allergenicity.

Peanut allergy usually develops in early childhood but can occasionally emerge later in life. It tends to be more persistent than milk and egg allergies. Infants with eczema and/or an existing egg allergy are more likely to develop a peanut allergy. The landmark clinical trial Learning Early About Peanut allergy (LEAP) demonstrated that the early introduction of peanut during the weaning of an infant onto solids can help to reduce the risk of peanut allergy in high-risk infants. Once peanut has been introduced into a child's diet, it is recommended to continue giving the equivalent of 1–2 teaspoons of peanut butter, 2–3 times per week to maintain their tolerance.

The follow-up study LEAP-ON found that for participants in whom peanuts had been introduced in the first year of life and continued regularly until 5 years of age, avoiding peanut afterwards for 12 months was not associated with an increase in the prevalence of peanut allergy. This suggests that consuming peanuts regularly during the early years provides long-term protection against peanut allergy in children at high risk of allergy, even with subsequent occasional periods of time without peanuts.

Although there is currently no cure for peanut allergy, oral immunotherapy has been used successfully to increase tolerance to peanut allergens. Very small amounts of peanut are introduced and the amount gradually increased until a target amount of the food is reached and maintained. This should only be carried out under medical supervision at a specialist centre due to the possibility of reactions occurring. The treatment requires a high level of commitment and ongoing consumption; although tolerance to good levels of peanut can be achieved, there may be a reversion to allergy if peanut stops being eaten.

Peanuts, soya, and lupin are included in the list of top 14 major food allergens in the UK and the European Union. If they are included in any food products, they must be highlighted on the food ingredients label. All other legumes and pulses are not highlighted but will still be listed in the ingredients. In the United States, peanut is the only legume that requires mandatory labelling. It is very uncommon to be allergic to all legumes but a person who is allergic to one food can become allergic to a similar food. This is called cross-reactivity. Most people are only allergic to one or a few legumes and can eat the others without problems. Unfortunately, allergies to foods not on the major allergen list are often not taken seriously due to a lack of understanding, but even those living with an allergy may be caught out by the variety of names that a particular legume can be called. The carob bean for example, botanically known as *Ceratonia siliqua* is also called the locust bean. Carob bean gum sold under the trade name Tragasol is widely used as a stabiliser and thickening agent in products as diverse as icing, infant foods, and toothpastes.

Legume allergies are more common in people from the Mediterranean region and some Asian and African countries, with lentils being the most common legume involved in allergic reactions in the Mediterranean area and India. A Turkish study showed that 50% of children with a lentil allergy developed tolerance before their teenage years. The prevalence of pea allergy is largely unknown but is thought to be rising. This may be linked to the rise of commercial food products containing pea-based ingredients such as pea protein and pea fibre. These are increasingly common additives in food as they can be a plant-based protein source, fat replacement, or used help to bind water. Pea protein isolate may now be found in many processed foods including meat products such as sausages and sliced cold meat, milk and dairy alternatives, soups, sauces, cereals, baked goods and gluten free foods. Even some ice creams promoted for children can contain pea protein. Pea protein is of particular concern for people with an allergy to peas because foods containing concentrated protein sources are more likely to trigger a severe reaction if accidentally consumed by someone with an allergy to that food.

If you have a legume allergy it is important to always check food labels as recipes may change. Question catering staff when eating out to check whether the allergen is an ingredient in the food you want to eat and ask whether there is a risk of cross-contamination when the food is prepared. If in doubt, take your business elsewhere. Always carry your medication with you and if you have an adrenaline auto-injector, ensure that it is in-date and you know how to use it. Do not be embarrassed about discussing your allergy with other people as this will help to spread awareness of the issues involved. Levels of understanding about allergies in the general public vary widely. There is often an underestimation of the condition's seriousness and widespread misconceptions. Many schools nowadays are often nut-free but may be less aware of other allergies. There are reports of schools not letting pupils have chocolate as one child is allergic to beans.

Foods for Special Purposes

The American physician and businessman John Harvey Kellogg (1852–1943), best known for his cornflakes, was the director of the

Battle Creek Sanatorium in Michigan. As an advocate of Fletcherism, a health practice named after Horace Fletcher (1849–1919) that encouraged chewing foods thoroughly to aid digestion, Kellogg began to grind foods for his sanatorium patients and created a high protein paste out of boiled peanuts. A former employee of Kellogg's, Ambrose Straub, patented a peanut-butter-making machine in 1903, making it possible to produce peanut butter from roasted peanuts on a large scale. Peanuts were widely promoted as a crop by agricultural researcher George Washington Carver as they reduced the need for fertilizers to improve soils depleted by repeated plantings of cotton. He suggested over 300 different uses for peanut, ranging from food items to industrial products.

Peanuts are ideally suited for use in therapeutic foods for famine relief due to their high fat and protein content. Ready-to-use therapeutic foods are supplied by the United Nations Children's Fund (UNICEF) for treatment of severe acute malnutrition and wasting in young children in places such as South Sudan, where malnutrition is a major contributor to high infant-mortality rates. Therapeutic foods are based on a peanut paste with added sugar, vegetable oil, and skim milk powder and are enriched with vitamins and minerals. Supplied in sachets with a two-year shelf life, they do not require refrigeration, added water, or any preparation and are suitable for children aged six months and older. Each sachet contains around 500 kilocalories and can be given without medical supervision, thus reducing the need for hospitalization. A similar product known as citadel spread was developed as a trail food for hikers. Citadel spread featured in Ed Garvey's 1971 book *Appalachian Hiker: Adventure of a Lifetime*. He suggested a combination of a jar of smooth peanut butter, the residual fat from 6–8 slices of bacon, some honey, and milk powder to provide an easily transportable source of nutrition. A vegetarian version can be made by substituting vegetable oil for the bacon fat. It will keep for at least three weeks unrefrigerated.

While rates of protein malnutrition can be high among elderly people admitted to hospitals, the majority of people in industrialized countries eat far more protein than they actually need. The average adult needs around 45–55 grams of protein per day but in the UK, consumption is usually between 75–100 grams. The modern food industry has been very successful in marketing protein-rich products to people who do not need them. High-protein bars, often based on pea or peanut protein, are widely promoted as handy, pre-packaged snacks. Soya bean and pea protein are often used in supplements aimed at bodybuilders or for sports nutrition. Research presented at the American Psychological Association's 2015 Annual Convention warned that overuse of protein supplements had become an emerging eating disorder that threatened health. Some protein powders have been found to be contaminated with heavy metals or toxins.

Flours made from chickpea, lupin and other pulses are gluten-free and so suitable for those with coeliac disease, although as with oats and other naturally gluten-free grains, there may sometimes be cross contamination issues during production or processing. Pulse flours are typically less expensive than nut flours, such as almond flour and hazelnut flour, and so are more budget friendly. Some pulse flours, such as those made from lupins, tend to have somewhat bitter flavours, but can be blended with other grain flours or used with herbs and spices to disguise the taste. Pulse flours absorb more moisture than other flours, so you need more liquid than usual if adapting recipes. Chickpea flour (gram flour) can be used as an egg substitute, particularly for making vegan omelettes, quiches, and for binding ingredients together in baking. To replace one egg, whisk together two tablespoons of chickpea flour with two tablespoons of water and one teaspoon of oil, then allow to stand for at least 5 minutes.

Health of the Planet

The current world population is estimated to be over 8 billion people. While growth is slowing, continued population increase puts pressure on world resources. According to the FAO, pulses offer great benefits for food security, nutrition, health, climate change, and biodiversity with potential to further achieve the 2030 Agenda for Sustainable Development. Including more plant foods and reducing animal foods in our diets is strongly advocated to reduce greenhouse gas emissions, water use, and deforestation. The nitrogen-fixing qualities of legumes can lessen the greenhouse gas emissions of arable production by lowering the need for artificial fertilisers. Drought-resistant legume species are particularly beneficial for dry climates where food security is often a challenge. Pulses can be dried and stored for relatively long periods of time without losing their nutritional value, allowing food reserves to be set aside in areas where it is scarce.

The 2025 planetary health diet (PHD) recommended by the Eat-Lancet Commission that was funded by the Wellcome Trust, aims to promote a sustainable food system which supplies healthy food to the expanding global population. The PHD is predominantly plant-based but may include modest amounts of fish, meat, and dairy. It encourages variation in vegetable and fruit intake but suggests limiting refined grains, highly processed foods, added sugars, and starchy vegetables. The report also calls for changes to the food system, including cutting food waste, greener farming practices and decent working conditions for agricultural workers. It is suggested that widespread adoption of such a diet could prevent 40,000 early deaths a day across the world. Michael Pollan, in his book *In Defense of Food: An Eater's Manifesto* (2008), summed up this way of eating in seven succinct words: 'Eat Food. Not too much. Mostly Plants.'

Italian research into agrifood wastes has been looking at using green bean and borlotti bean fibres as part of the quest to develop more sustainable clothing. Using fibres of vegetable origin has benefits in achieving better waste management, saving on disposal costs, and also providing high value products. Biofabrics and food-derived garments can be composted when they are no longer used, unlike petroleum-derived fabrics, enabling them to return to the soil.

The food of a region or country and its history may be used to promote nationalism and national identity. While this can be a positive thing, it may involve arguments between regions when a particular dish is claimed by one region and considered to have been appropriated by another. Such culinary nationalism is sometimes termed gastronationalism and has been criticized as an example of banal nationalism. Food and social inclusion can be deeply linked, with shared meals helping to build a sense of community. Inclusive practices like community kitchens with diverse menus are important for bringing people together. Indian food, for example, is today considered part of British culture, with chicken tikka masala often described as an 'adopted national dish.'

The first Indian restaurant in the United Kingdom, the Hindoostane Coffee House, was opened in 1810 by the surgeon and entrepreneur Dean Mahomed (1759–1851). Mahomed, born in the city of Patna to a Shia Muslim family was a former captain in the British East India Company's Bengal Army. He advertised 'dinners, composed of genuine Hindoostane dishes' with orders for home delivery 'punctually attended to.' Indian food had been popular in Britain before Mahomed opened his Coffee House. Hannah Glasse's 1747 cookbook *The Art of Cookery Made Plain and Simple* provided recipes for chicken curry and pilaus. An advertisement in the Public Advertiser on 6 December 1773 announced that the 'Mistress of Norris Street Coffee House, Haymarket' could supply 'true Indian curey paste' and provided a home delivery service for 'ready dressed curey and rice, also India pilaws, to any part of the town.'

There is evidence that sharing food and exchanging recipes across cultures may help lead to a more inclusive and tolerant society. A 2025 study led by Dr. Rodolfo Leyva of the University of Birmingham consisting of more than 1,000 white British adults found a correlation between enjoyment of international cuisine and positive attitudes towards immigrants. Those people who regularly consumed Indian, Turkish, Chinese, Thai, Caribbean or Spanish foods were less likely to perceive immigrants as 'cultural or economic threats' and had a decreased likelihood of voting for anti-immigrant politicians. The research implied that these attitudes were not simply because the diners were more open in the first place but that tolerant attitudes were largely explained by increased positive contact with individuals from different cultures. Leyva suggests that, 'Restaurants or food stalls tend to offer welcoming environments that facilitate natural, friendly interactions with people from immigrant communities.' The positive associations created by the experience of eating good ethnic foods can become firmly embedded in memory, leading to the formation of a favourable relationship with the respective culture, so going out to enjoy some dosa at your local Indian restaurant may have many surprising benefits.

Chapter 6
IN THE KITCHEN

I eat my peas with honey;
I've done it all my life.
It makes the peas taste funny,
But it keeps them on the knife.

Attributed to Ogden Nash (1902–1971)

Nash's ditty advocating peas with honey is probably the most well-known of pulse poems, but as a recipe it is somewhat inexact. The contemporary American poet Susan Terris complained in her poem 'Dish of Mashed Peas' (2018) about vague recipe instructions, although as happiness would be granted had she left her finished dish outdoors in the moonlight, it may well have been worth some experimentation. The earliest known written recipes were found inscribed on clay tablets from ancient Mesopotamia. Written in the extinct language Akkadian, these contain lists of ingredients for preparing various stews, such as lamb, garlic, and barley combined with herbs and spices. Terris would definitely not approve of the cooking instructions either, which are, to say the least, imprecise. The recipes were probably intended as aide memoires for experienced cooks.

The fourteenth-century English cookbook known as *The Forme of Cury*, has a title that roughly equates to The Method of Cooking, 'cury' being a word derived from the Old French *queuerie*, meaning 'cookery.' It is thought to have been compiled by the master cooks of King Richard II. It includes recipes for fava beans, which were the only type widely available in medieval Europe, and features the dishes 'Benes yfryed' (fried beans) and 'Drawen benes' (a mashed bean pottage coloured with saffron). The English writer Eliza Acton (1799–1859) was possibly the first cookery writer to itemise recipe ingredients and include cooking times. Fictionalised in Annabel Abbs' novel *The Language of Food* (2022), Acton was a poet before turning to food writing and published her first book of modern cookery in 1845. Her father, John Acton, had been declared bankrupt in 1827 and she was very conscious of cooking within a budget and adapting recipes to one's means. Her 'poor author's pudding' is a simple bread-and-butter pudding, while the more extravagant 'publisher's pudding' includes cognac, cream, almonds from Jordan, and dried fruit. She was keen to show how the cuisine of other nations, such as curries and chutneys, could be adapted and enjoyed by everyone.

If you have learned to cook by watching a family member in the kitchen, then your traditional foods, the equivalent perhaps of my shepherd's pie and apple crumble, are probably made without conscious referral to a recipe. However, for most of us for whom food is an abiding interest, your home may have at least one shelf full of cookery books, albeit nowadays this may be in digital form. I love Felicity Cloake's search for perfect recipes but mostly what I cook are heavily adapted versions of recipes, based on what happens to be in the garden, in the cupboard, or in the bottom of the fridge. I read recipe books for interest and inspiration and as a guide when preparing something new but will rarely follow a recipe to the letter. Personally, I tend more towards Nash's imprecision than Terris' need for exactitude. My most used cook book, *The Good Housekeeping Cookery Book* (1985), bought when I was a student dietitian, is now fondly referred to as 'my cooked book' as it bears the circular scars from the time I put it down on a hot hob ring. When I bought it, I loved that the recipes had been thoroughly tested and felt authoritative.

The writing does lack that personal touch which can turn a recipe book into exemplary bedtime reading. However, the blank pages at the back are now full of my scribbled essential extra recipes, such Wellington squares, lemon polenta cake and black bean brownies, in flagrant disregard of my lifelong conviction that writing in a book is sacrilegious.

Today, the availability of ingredients and recipes can seem infinite and that wealth of choice can make selecting something for supper after a busy day at work somewhat stressful. Do not feel guilty about reaching for a can of baked beans to put on some toast or reheating a simple mashed bean pottage as soothing options, but adding some halved cherry tomatoes, roughly chopped bell peppers, or chorizo and a teaspoon of harissa paste, pesto, or indeed honey, to tinned beans will enable you to turn what has become a British staple into something more individual.

Purchase, Preparation and Storage

Pulses such as beans, lentils, and chickpeas can be readily purchased from most food shops, supermarkets, and online retailers in both dried and canned forms. Specialist suppliers with a high turnover are likely to have fresher stock. Pulses have a long shelf life, so are useful items to store in the cupboard. If stored in a cool, dry place, dried pulses will keep for at least a year or two and some will still be edible almost indefinitely. Commercial storage aims to keep moisture content below 14% and temperature below 20°C (68°F). Pulses harvested under wet conditions and insufficiently dried may be vulnerable to microbial spoilage by moulds, bacteria, and yeasts. Bean weevils sometimes infest stored pulses. The eggs are almost invisible to the naked eye, so may not be spotted but the olive-brown adults are approximately 4–5 mm (0.2″) long and can be seen without magnification. They often 'play dead,' dropping to the ground when disturbed. They do not carry disease so accidentally eating them should do no harm, although it is not recommended in case of any potential contamination with pesticides. If you do not mind the thought of some additional protein, freezing any potentially infested beans will kill any wildlife, just rinse and cook them thoroughly afterwards.

Packets of pulses rescued from the back of the cupboard that have passed their 'best before' date may still be used. Tannins in the seed coats of some coloured seeds such as puy lentils can oxidize over time, causing discolouration and if they have been exposed to light, some beans' colour will fade. All vitamins will decay over time, with the water-soluble vitamins C and B being most sensitive to environmental factors including moisture, heat, light, and oxygen. Pulses stored too long will therefore lose some of their nutritional benefits. Oxidation of unsaturated fatty acids such as linoleic and linolenic acids within the seeds can result in the development of off flavours during storage. Long-stored seeds become harder as they age and will therefore need longer rehydration times. They will also take longer to cook, becoming tougher and less creamy in texture than fresher beans. Eventually the seeds will no longer rehydrate but can still be used if ground into bean flour.

All dried pulses, except lentils and split peas, are usually soaked in water to rehydrate before cooking. Typically, three cups of water are needed for every one cup of dried peas/beans. Allow them to soak for around 4–6 hours or overnight in a bowl or pan and then rinse them in clean water. Soaking is said to reduce any anti-nutrient factors and rinse off the starches that can cause foaming when boiling. It should also reduce the cooking time and save on fuel. If you have not planned your bean dinner a day ahead, you can 'quick soak' pulses by covering them in water, bring them to a boil for a couple of minutes, then turn off the heat and leave to stand for an hour. Many cooks argue against pre-soaking, saying it is unnecessary and reduces flavour, but I suspect few of us have a palate refined enough to tell the difference in a blind challenge.

Many older recipe books suggest adding bicarbonate of soda during soaking to help soften pulses and ensure they cook more quickly. It does have a high sodium content so is not recommended for regular use but can be helpful if you live in a hard water area as it increases the pH of the soaking water, allowing water to penetrate the cell walls of the seeds more quickly. It is commonly used for the marrowfat 'mushy' peas of traditional fish and chip shops.

Unfortunately, it can make the pulses somewhat slimy with a soapy taste, so do not use more than one teaspoon bicarb (5 g) per 500 g (1 lb) pulses.

To cook, cover rehydrated pulses with water in a saucepan or stockpot. Bring them to a boil and boil for ten minutes, then lower the heat and simmer until tender. Keeping the lid on the pan while cooking gives a more consistent temperature and reduces cooking times. Once tender, they can easily be squashed between finger and thumb or mashed with a fork against the side of the pan. Peas and small beans typically take around 45 minutes of simmering while larger beans may need to simmer for as long as 2 hours. A pressure cooker will speed up the cooking considerably. Once cooked, they are ready to be used in your recipe or can be kept in an airtight container in the fridge for 3–5 days, ideally covered in their cooking liquid to prevent them from drying out. Cooked beans/chickpeas freeze very well, so it is worth cooking more than you need and freezing some (strained of their cooking liquid) to save time on another occasion.

Notes for Recipes

Most of the quantities given are easy going and conversions between imperial and metric measurements fairly random. Some people get worried about the difference between UK and US measurements in recipes but actually it is rarely significant. For those who like exactitude, a UK cup capacity is 250 ml, whereas the standard US cup is 237 ml, generally rounded up to 240 ml (8 oz). If you are a pharmacist or an engineer a difference of that magnitude will be important. When cooking I would suggest you just get granny's china cup from the back of the cupboard and use that. Of course, if granny has left you an antique eighteenth-century porcelain tea bowl the capacity may be a mere 90 ml compared with that of a typical modern mug of around 300 ml.

1 cup dried beans is equivalent to about 3 cups cooked beans.

1 × 400 g (14 oz) can of beans is equivalent to around ½ cup dried beans or 1.5 cups cooked beans.

I have included a rough guide to how many servings you can expect but obviously this will vary depending on whether you are feeding fussy toddlers or a party of hungry hikers.

For recipes that require stock, you can use the results of the long slow-cooking of a meat bone or chicken carcass with assorted vegetables, herbs and a Parmesan rind, that will produce a rich flavourful basis to the recipe, but there is no shame in using a low-salt stock cube. I rarely add salt when I am cooking as most of us have far more salt than we need in our diet. I do keep a container in the cupboard in case it is requested by guests or needed for de-icing the back step in winter. You can obviously season to taste. Though you can train your taste buds to get used to less salt and thereby better able to distinguish other flavours, by gradually reducing the amount of salt you add.

All ovens will have their own idiosyncrasies and you will get to know how your own works and whether to adjust temperatures. You may find you need to knock ten minutes off the cooking time or leave things in for a bit longer.

Soups and Starters

Monastery Soup

After going on a pilgrimage to see the snowdrops of the Black Sea coast of Turkey and Georgia, I bought a copy of Caroline Eden's fascinating cookery/travelogue *Black Sea: Dispatches and Recipes—Through Darkness and Light* (2018). Her recipe for monastery soup is a variant on the traditional *bob chorba* or Bulgarian bean soup which would be served during lent in Bulgaria's monasteries. She reports that it would be traditionally cooked in a large earthenware pot, but it works just as well in any heavy-bottomed saucepan. We were served similar, satisfying soups in Georgia, along with fantastic bread. It was written that man cannot live on bread alone, but with Georgian bread and this soup you could live very well indeed. Committed carnivores may want to sauté some slices of smoked sausage to add to the soup.

Serves 4

Ingredients

- 2 tbsp vegetable oil (or melted butter)
- 1 large red bell pepper, diced
- 1 large onion, diced
- 2 medium carrots
- 200 g (1½ cups) precooked/canned white beans, rinsed and drained
- 200 g (1½ cups) precooked/canned kidney beans, rinsed and drained
- 750 ml (3 cups) vegetable stock
- 2 tsp paprika
- 1 tsp dried or 1 tbsp fresh summer savory (*Satureja hortensis*)
- 1 pinch freshly ground black pepper
- Chopped spearmint and 2 tbsp sour cream to garnish, if liked

Peel the carrots and cut into slices. Cook carrots, onion, and pepper together in the oil over a medium heat for 5–10 minutes, until the onion is softened. Add the paprika and black pepper and continue cooking for a couple of minutes, then add the stock, beans, and the savory. Bring the pot to a boil and then turn the heat down and simmer for 20 minutes, until the carrots are soft.

Pour into bowls, garnish with the optional sour cream and spearmint, and serve with good bread.

Lablabi

In the early 1980s, the Tunisian tourist board ran a series of TV adverts suggesting that 'in your dreams you've been to Tunisia.' I was inspired to go for real and loved the architecture, the sunshine, the camel-riding, and the street food, particularly *brik*, a fried egg pastry, lightly cooked so that the egg yolk runs down your chin as you eat. Lablabi is a traditional Tunisian soup based on chickpeas in a spicy garlic and cumin flavoured broth. It is usually served over chunks of stale bread and often topped with a poached egg. Fresh bread can get a little too mushy, so if you do not have any stale bread, drizzle some oil over fresh chunks of bread and toast/roast/fry them lightly beforehand. An essential ingredient is harissa paste, the hot chilli pepper paste popular throughout North Africa. UNESCO includes harissa as part of Tunisia's Intangible Cultural Heritage. You can make your own, but jars of prepared paste are readily available in supermarkets.

Serves 4

Ingredients

1 × 400 g (14 oz) can or 3 cups precooked chickpeas
750 ml (3 cups) chicken or vegetable stock
3 tbsp olive oil
4 cloves of garlic, crushed
1 tbsp harissa
1 tsp ground cumin
1 lemon
½ tsp black pepper
2 tbsp capers, drained
Stale bread, torn into bite-sized chunks

Fry the garlic and spices in the oil. Add the chickpeas, stock, and the juice of half the lemon, bring to the boil and simmer for 15–20 minutes. Blend about half of the cooked chickpeas with a cup of the cooking liquid, return to the pan, and stir to give a creamy texture. Divide your bread between serving bowls and then ladle the soup over the chunks. Serve with wedges of the remaining half lemon and some extra harissa for those who like things spicy. Sprinkle with the capers. The capers are traditional, although, as Nora Ephron noted in her novel *Heartburn* (1983), 'the truth is that any dish that tastes good with capers in it, tastes even better with capers not in it.'

Fasolada

The best time to visit Greece is in autumn when the hillsides are studded with pink cyclamen, starry autumn narcissi, and, if you time it right, the golden goblets of *Sternbergia*. If you cannot make it to Greece, you can nonetheless fuel a good stomp through autumn leaves with a sustaining bowl of this Greek white bean soup. Recipes vary considerably, often including tomatoes and other vegetables such as carrots and sometimes cured meat such as basturma. Lima/butter beans can be used instead of white beans.

Serves 4

Ingredients

2 × 400 g (14 oz) can or 6 cups precooked cannelloni or other white beans
1 large onion, chopped
2 cloves of garlic, crushed
4 stalks of celery, chopped
750 ml (3 cups) chicken or vegetable stock
2 tbsp olive oil
1 tsp dried oregano
1 tsp ground cumin
1 tsp paprika
Zest and juice of 1 small lemon

Gently cook the onion and pepper in the oil for about 5 minutes. Then add the garlic, celery, and oregano and cook for another 5 minutes, stirring regularly. Add the stock, beans, and spices and bring to a boil. Reduce the heat, cover, and simmer for 10 minutes. Ladle 2 cups of the soup into a bowl and blend until smooth, then return this to the pan. Add the lemon. Simmer for another 5 minutes, then serve.

Garbure

Garbure is not fast food. This is a slow, comforting, rustic soup which comes from Gascony in the southwest region of France. The important ingredients are broad or white beans and savoy cabbage but there are many variations and a variety of other vegetables can be used. Nowadays, most use a smoked ham hock for the meat but goose or duck confit are traditional. Stale bread may be added if available. It is said that a garbure is only truly authentic if it is thick enough for a ladle to stand upright in it. Garbure can be served as a soup but is substantial enough to be a main course. In France, it is often served as two courses: first the broth with the vegetables and then the meat as a main course with a salad. If you are going to invest the time in cooking something slow, it is worth making enough for two meals or inviting people round.

Serves 8

Ingredients

- 250 g (9 oz) dried broad or white beans (such as Tarbais, navy, or cannellini), soaked overnight
- 1 kg (2.2 lb) ham hock
- 50 g (3.5 tbsp) butter (or duck fat, or olive oil)
- 1 large onion, peeled and studded with 6 cloves
- 2 large carrots, peeled and sliced
- 3 medium potatoes, peeled and diced
- 1 large turnip, peeled and diced
- ¼ of a savoy cabbage, shredded
- 2 cloves of garlic, crushed
- 4 bay leaves
- 1 tsp dried thyme
- Ground black pepper, to taste

Cook the ham hock by placing it in a large stock pot with the beans, onion, bay leaves, and thyme. Add enough water to just barely cover it, bring it to a boil, and boil for 10 minutes, then reduce the heat, cover, and simmer for an hour.

In a separate pan, fry the carrots, turnip and garlic in the butter or fat over medium heat and then add this to the meat pot. Cover and simmer gently for another hour, then stir in the cabbage and simmer for 30 minutes. Add the potatoes and cook for another 30 minutes until tender. Fish out the bay leaves and remove the hock to a cutting board. Take off the skin and fat and shred the flesh with two forks. Remove the onion from the pot. Discard the cloves but chop the onion and return it to the pot along with the meat. Give everything a good stir then serve as one course or two.

Shorabet Adas

There are numerous variations on the basic red lentil soup. Shorabet adas is a Lebanese one. The Anatolian red lentil soup (*Mercimek Çorbası*) is similar but uses Aleppo pepper, cumin, and coriander for heat and earthiness. This is one of the recipes that is easier to measure with cups rather than getting out the scales. Use teacups if you want the soup for a starter or mugs if it is intended as a meal.

Serves 8

Ingredients

- 2 cups (400 g) red lentils
- 8 cups (2 litres) stock or water
- 1 large onion, roughly chopped
- 1 carrot, chopped
- 2 tbsp olive oil
- 2 cloves of garlic, crushed
- 1 tsp ground cumin
- Ground black pepper, to taste
- 1 lemon

Fry the onions, garlic, and carrots with some black pepper for around 5 minutes over medium heat. Add the lentils and cumin and stir. Add the stock and bring the pot to a boil, then simmer gently for around half an hour. Use a hand blender or food processor to blend this to a smooth texture and then serve with chunks of bread and lemon wedges.

Romanian Beaten Beans

This traditional Romanian white bean dip is known as fasole bătută which literally means 'beaten beans' as that is how they are traditionally prepared: beaten with a rolling pin. It is a smooth and garlicky white bean paste topped with caramelized onions.

SERVES 8

Ingredients

250 g (8 oz) dried white beans
2 large onions
2 bay leaves
4 tbsp sunflower or other vegetable oil
3 cloves garlic, grated
2 onions
2 tbsp tomato paste
1 tsp honey or brown sugar
2 tsp paprika

Rinse the beans, cover with water, and leave to soak overnight. The next day, rinse them again and place in saucepan with half an onion and the bay leaves. Cover with water, bring to boil, and boil for 10 minutes, then reduce the temperature and simmer for around an hour. Drain the beans but reserve the cooking water. Discard the bay leaves and blend the beans, garlic, and the half onion with 2 tablespoons of the oil and about 3 tablespoons cooking liquid. Add more cooking liquid if required to get a smooth but firm consistency, like thick Greek yogurt.

Slice the remaining onions and fry in 2 tablespoons of oil until transparent. Add the tomato paste, honey, and paprika and stir until slightly caramelized.

Transfer the beans to a serving dish and top with the onions. This can be served hot as a starter or side dish or as a cold dip with bread.

Lentil Puree

Fans of the British cookery writer Annabel Karmel will probably be familiar with her lentil puree which has now served as a weaning food for a whole generation of babies. You do not have to stop eating lentil puree once you have grown up of course, and this version is a good way to use some of that post-Halloween glut of pumpkin flesh.

SERVES 4 (OR LOTS OF BABY-SIZED PORTIONS)

Ingredients

1 tbsp olive oil
½ onion, diced
1 garlic clove, minced
1 medium carrot, peeled and diced
½ stalk celery, chopped
½ red bell pepper, chopped
100 g (½ cup) red lentils, rinsed
250 g (9 oz) pumpkin or squash, peeled and chopped
375 ml (1½ cups) chicken/vegetable stock (or water)
1 tsp paprika

Gently fry the onion, garlic, carrots, and celery for approximately 5–10 minutes until softened. Add the red pepper and pumpkin and continue cooking for another minute or two. Pour in the lentils and stock, bring to a boil, then reduce the heat and let it simmer for approximately 20 minutes. Use a hand blender or food processor to puree the mixture until smooth and creamy. Serve with pita bread.

Florentine Pea Baskets

I first came across a recipe for *cestini di piselli* (baskets of fresh peas) in the book *Florentines: A Tuscan Feast* (1992), a celebration of the art of Giovanna Garzoni with foreword and recipes by the Italian writer Lorenza de' Medici who died in 2024 at the age of 98. The Italians are wonderfully inventive and there are many variations offered online for how to make edible baskets, including flattened slices of bread moulded into muffin tins and baked or using filo pastry, but de' Medici's version made with a semolina batter is delightful. I like the addition of pine nuts and grated hard cheese, such as Parmesan, to the peas but you can stick with simple buttered peas if you prefer.

Serves 6

Ingredients

- 500 ml (2 cups) milk
- 150 g (1 cup) semolina
- 30 g (2 tbsp) butter
- 2 eggs
- 150 g (1.5 cups) dried breadcrumbs
- Oil for deep frying
- 200 g (1.5 cups) boiled green peas
- 15 g (2 tbsp) pine nuts, toasted
- Grated Parmesan cheese to taste

Bring the milk to a boil in a saucepan and pour in the semolina while stirring, then cook over a low heat for 20 minutes. Add half the butter, stir until melted, and remove from the heat and allow to cool. Stir in one egg. Using your hands roll the semolina paste into 6 balls and make a hollow in the middle of each with your thumbs. Beat the remaining egg with a fork and dip the semolina baskets in the egg, then cover them lightly with breadcrumbs. Heat the oil to around 180°C (350°F), add the baskets, and fry until golden. Drain on paper towels.

Melt the remaining butter in a small saucepan, add the peas and pine nuts and warm through for few minutes. Arrange baskets on a serving dish or individual saucers, fill with buttered peas and pine nuts, sprinkle with Parmesan, and serve.

Main Courses

Babgulyás

A goulash (gulyas) is somewhere between a soup and a stew in consistency but is always richly flavoured. The most familiar goulash to non-Hungarians is the beef-based version, with vegetables as the secondary interest. With babgulyás, beans provide the main protein source with some meat added chiefly for flavour. A Hungarian friend gave me a jar of red Hungarian wax peppers which is her secret ingredient when making goulash, but you can use a bell pepper if necessary. Hungarian paprika is sweeter and more subtle in flavour than many Spanish versions. Ideally the pork would come from a Hungarian mangalitsa. This is a rare breed of pig related to the Lincolnshire Curly Coat pig, which became extinct in the United Kingdom in the 1970s. Mangalitsa lard is said to be lighter than lard from other pigs and melts at a lower temperature because it contains more unsaturated fat. The list of ingredients may look intimidatingly long but you can be flexible with what you use and the cooking is simplicity itself.

Serves 6

Ingredients

- 400 g (2 cups) mixed dried beans, soaked overnight then rinsed and drained
- 2 tbsp oil (or duck fat or lard if you have it)
- 2 medium onions, chopped
- 1 small celeriac, or two stalks celery
- 4 cloves garlic, crushed
- 2 carrots, chopped
- 1 small turnip, if available peeled and diced
- 8–12 small firm new potatoes, halved (or 1–2 medium potatoes, chopped)
- 1 large bell pepper, seeds and stem removed and diced (or a couple of Hungarian wax peppers, diced)
- 2 large tomatoes, diced
- 2 tbsp tomato paste
- 3 tbsp Hungarian paprika
- 1 tsp dried thyme
- 2 tsp dried marjoram
- 1 tsp crushed caraway seeds
- 3 bay leaves
- 1 tsp freshly ground black pepper
- 500 g (1 lb) leftover pork belly, a large pork chop, or smoked sausage, cut into bite sized chunks
- 1500 ml (6 cups) chicken or vegetable stock

Heat the oil or lard in a large saucepan over medium heat and fry the onions for 5 minutes or so until soft. Add the meat and stir to seal, searing it all on sides. Add all the other ingredients and stir. Bring everything to a boil for 10 minutes, then reduce the heat, and simmer slowly for 1½–2 hours. Fish out the bay leaves and serve in bowls with a large dollop of sour cream on top and fresh crispy bread to mop the juices.

Salt Pork with Puy Lentils

For an authentic French recipe for *petit sale aux lentilles* (salt pork with lentils) I was advised to see the website of the Marie Claire magazine. Their method suggests putting the rinsed lentils in a 'marmite' which caused me some confusion until I realised that a marmite is a traditional French cooking pot, made of earthenware or metal, as well as a British sticky savoury spread. Montbéliard sausage is recommended, which is a smoked pork sausage using 'porc de Franche-Comté' and spices including caraway, garlic, pepper and juniper, but you may have to improvise.

Serves 6

Ingredients

- 1 kg (2.2 lb) salt pork
- 200 g (8 oz) smoked sausage, thickly sliced
- 50 g (3.5 tbsp) unsalted butter
- 500 g (2.5 cups) puy lentils
- 1 fat carrot, diced
- 1 small celeriac or 2 stalks celery, diced
- 2 onions, diced
- 1 tsp sage
- 1 tsp rosemary
- 1 tsp parsley, chopped
- 3 bay leaves
- 3 sprigs thyme
- Black pepper, to taste

Soak the pork in a bowl of cold water in the fridge for about 4–6 hours to remove some of the excess salt. Drain and rinse.

Put the pork in a large saucepan/stockpot/marmite; cover with water; add the carrots, onion, celeriac, and herbs and simmer gently for an hour and a half. Remove the pork from the pot and set aside to rest. Rinse the lentils, then add them to the pork liquid and the vegetables, along with the sliced sausage. Simmer for about 20 minutes until the lentils are tender but not mushy, adding more water if necessary. Cut the meat into chunky slices. Drain the lentil mixture and transfer to a serving dish. Arrange the meat on top and put it in the oven to reheat.

Turkish White Bean Stew

Kuru fasülye is a Turkish stew made from beans cooked in a thick buttery sauce. It is usually served with rice or big chunks of crusty sourdough bread and 'turşu' (torshi) which are pickled vegetables such as Guindilla peppers and gherkins, wedges of lemon, and a scatter of fresh parsley.

Serves 4

Ingredients

- 500 g (2 cups) dried white beans (such as navy beans, haricot, or cannellini), soaked overnight
- 400 g (14 oz) can chopped tomatoes
- 50 g (3.5 tbsp) butter
- 1 small onion, finely chopped
- 3 cloves garlic, crushed
- 2 bay leaves
- 1 tsp black pepper
- 2 tbsp tomato paste
- 1 tbsp harissa/red pepper paste or a finely chopped chilli pepper

Drain the beans and put into a heavy-bottomed pan. Cover with water, add the bay leaves, and bring to the boil. Boil for 10 minutes, skim off any froth, then lower the heat, cover, and simmer for 1–1½ hours until soft, adding extra water if needed. Melt the butter in a separate pan and over

Fig. 37. Turkish white bean stew.

medium heat, fry the onion and garlic for 5 minutes then add tomato paste, stirring until thickened. Add the harissa or chillies and canned tomatoes and cook for another couple of minutes. Add the beans and simmer for 20–30 minutes.

Pea Risotto

My all-time favourite risotto is the Milanese, which is custard yellow, flavoured with saffron, and ideally served outside one of the many restaurants overlooking the Gothic extravagance that is Milan Cathedral. However, I do also love the simplicity of a plate of green, so a pea risotto is always very welcome. The pea pods can be used to make the stock. If you have grown the peas yourself and have some pea shoots available, they will make a pretty garnish to the dish. If you like, you can add chopped ham or bacon lardons.

Serves 4 as main or 6 as a starter

Ingredients

- 300 g (2.25 cups) boiled fresh or frozen peas
- 1.5 litres (6 cups) hot vegetable stock
- 350 g (1.75 cups) risotto rice
- 200 ml (7 fl oz) white wine
- 25 g / 1 oz Parmesan cheese
- 50 g (3.5 tbsp) butter
- 1 onion, finely chopped
- 1 tsp fresh mint, chopped

Melt the butter in a large pan, add the onion, and cook gently for about 10 minutes until soft. Meanwhile, blend about a third of the peas with a ladleful of stock with a hand blender or in a food processor to make a purée. Stir the rice into the onion, increase the heat somewhat, and let the rice sizzle for a minute or two. Pour in the wine and stir until completely absorbed. Add the stock a ladleful at a time, stirring until the rice has a smooth creamy consistency. Set aside a good 20–30 minutes for this; you should not rush a risotto! Stir in the puréed peas, remaining whole peas, Parmesan, and mint, then turn off the heat and leave to stand for a few minutes. Give the risotto a final stir, spoon into shallow bowls, and top with pea shoots or a drizzle of olive oil.

Paella Valenciana

Some people get very heated about food and certainly the recipes typical of a region often provoke intense argument. An article in the 2022 *International Journal of Gastronomy and Food Science* reported on Rafael Vidal's search for the authentic paella of the Valencia region of Spain. He believes the traditional recipe should have ten basic ingredients: Valencian rice, olive oil, rabbit, chicken, saffron or a substitute, tomato, flat green beans, lima (butter) beans, salt, and water. The yellow colour usually comes from saffron, but turmeric and pot marigold (*Calendula*) can be used instead. Artichoke hearts and stems may be used in season. Most paella cooks use the short-grained bomba rice cultivated in the eastern parts of Spain. It has a high content of amylose starch and can absorb two or three times its volume in water without bursting, so it does not become sticky. Ideally, paella would be cooked outside on an open fire using orange or pine wood but it is just as nutritious and tasty if you use your kitchen hob. If you do not have a special paella pan, use the widest frying pan you have.

Serves 4

Ingredients

- 400 g (2 cups) paella rice (e.g., Bomba, Senia, or Calasparra)
- 750 g (1.5 lb) meat—use a combination of chicken thighs, rabbit pieces, and pork, depending on availability (you can add snails if you wish)
- 200 g (8 oz) precooked or canned lima beans
- 8–10 pods flat green or runner beans
- 1 large tomato, finely chopped
- 50 ml (scant ¼ cup) olive oil
- 1500 ml (6 cups) chicken stock or water
- 2 cloves garlic
- 2 teaspoons paprika
- 1 pinch saffron (about 10 threads)
- 1 tsp salt

Heat the oil in the pan over medium heat. Add the meat and cook for about 20 minutes until golden brown. Push the meat toward the outside of the pan, add the green beans, and cook for a couple of minutes. Move the beans to the edge of the pan and add the garlic. Sauté for a few seconds and then add the butter beans and sauté for about 1 minute. Add the paprika, then add the tomato and saffron and gently stir everything together. Add the stock and bring to a rapid boil for about 10 minutes and then lower the heat and simmer without stirring for another 15–20 minutes. Towards the end of the cooking time, you should hear a crackling sound coming from the bottom layer of rice which occurs when it is caramelizing, making what the Spanish call *socarrat*, a tasty, crispy crust. Remove the paella from the heat. Cover with a clean tea towel and let it rest for 5 minutes, then serve.

Black Eye Bean (Chowli) Curry

Thanks to Rachel and Malcolm for their chowli curry recipe. I have added rough quantities, although as Rachel says, when Malcolm makes it 'he just throws them in,' which may well be easier if you are of Indian heritage.

Serves 4

Ingredients

- 2 × 400 g can (6 cups) precooked black eyed beans
- 500 g (1 lb) new potatoes, diced
- 1 large onion, finely diced
- 1 tbsp oil, melted butter or ghee
- 1 tsp ginger and garlic paste
- 1 tsp cumin powder
- 1 tsp coriander powder
- 1 tsp garam masala powder
- 1 tsp chilli powder
- 1 tsp turmeric powder
- 1 vegetable stock cube
- 2 large tomatoes, chopped or 1 × 400 g (14 oz) tin tomatoes
- 400 ml (14 fl oz) can coconut milk

Boil the potatoes for 10–15 minutes. Meanwhile, fry the onion in the oil on medium heat, add the spices and ginger and garlic paste and stir until it forms a masala paste (you may need to add a small amount of water). Mix in the stock cube, then add the tomatoes together with the potatoes and simmer for around 20 minutes. Add the beans and the coconut milk and simmer together for another 5–10 minutes. Serve with rice or naan.

Punjabi Chole Masala

Chole masala is a chickpea curry from the state of Punjab in north-western India, cooked with onions, tomatoes, and lots of spices. Traditionally eaten with bhatura, a deep-fried flatbread, it is a popular street food. It uses a special blend of spices known by the same name as the dish. Felicity Cloake writes that the holy trinity of ingredients are onions, ginger, and green chillies. She does not use the tea bag but I like the added depth of colour it gives.

You can buy chole masala powder ready mixed or make your own:

Ingredients

- 2 tbsp coriander seeds
- 1 tbsp cumin seeds
- 1 tbsp dried pomegranate seeds
- 1 tsp black peppercorn
- 2 black cardamoms
- 8 cloves
- 3–4 dried red chilies
- 2-inch cinnamon stick
- 1 tsp ginger powder
- 1 tsp dried mango powder

Stir all the whole spices in a pan on medium heat for around 5 minutes until they are fragrant and light golden in colour. Allow to cool then grind into a powder with a spice grinder or mortar and pestle. Then stir in the ginger and mango powders.

Serves 4

Ingredients

- 1 × 400 g (14 oz) can or 3 cups precooked chickpeas
- 400 g large tomatoes, or 1 × 400 g (14 oz) can chopped tomatoes
- 1 teabag of black Indian tea
- 1 tbsp vegetable oil or melted butter/ghee
- 1 large onion, finely chopped
- 3 garlic cloves, peeled
- 25 g (1 oz) ginger root
- 30 g (1 oz) fresh coriander (cilantro)
- 3 green chillies, finely chopped
- 1 tsp ground turmeric
- 2 tsp chole masala (as above)
- 1 tbsp lemon juice

Put the chickpeas in a pan with the teabag and add 500 ml water. Bring to a simmer and cook for 5 minutes then turn off the heat.

In a separate large pan, heat the oil over medium heat, add the onion, and cook until softened, stirring regularly. Use a mortar and pestle or hand blender to mash the garlic, ginger, fresh coriander, and chillies into a paste. Add this to the pan and cook for a couple of minutes, then add the rest of the spices and cook for a couple more minutes. Discard the teabag then stir the chickpeas, their cooking water, and the tomatoes into the onion and spice mixture. Bring back to the boil, then turn down the heat and simmer for 20 minutes or until thickened. Stir in the lemon juice, then serve with bhatura, rice, or another flatbread.

Usal

Usal is a classic Indian dish from the Maharashtra region consisting of beans in a spicy coconut sauce. Like the popular Mumbai street-food *misal pav*, made from moth beans, usal uses sprouted beans which reduces the phytate content and increases the vitamin C levels. They will need sprouting 2–3 days before you cook the curry: rinse the beans then soak in water overnight, then drain and rinse morning and evening for another 24–48 hours. You are just aiming for small roots, not the lengthy sprouts of Chinese cuisine. You can use any type of oil (i.e., olive, vegetable, sunflower, mustard, etc.) in this dish.

Ingredients

For the masala paste

- 2 tbsp oil
- ½ onion, sliced
- 3 cloves garlic, crushed
- 25 g (1 oz) ginger root
- 2 tbsp desiccated coconut
- 4 tbsp water

Heat the oil and add the onion, garlic, and ginger. Sauté for a few minutes then add the coconut and cook until it turns golden brown. Cool and then blend with the water to make a smooth paste.

Serves 4

Ingredients

- 2 tbsp oil
- 1 onion, finely chopped
- 1 tsp mustard
- 1 tsp cumin
- 1 tsp turmeric
- 1 tsp chilli powder
- Masala paste, as above
- 1 tomato, finely chopped
- 400 g (2 cups) mung beans, sprouted
- 2 tbsp fresh coriander (cilantro), finely chopped

Heat the oil in a large pan over a low heat and add the mustard, cumin, and onion and sauté until it changes colour slightly. Add turmeric, chilli powder, and masala paste and cook for a few minutes. Add the tomato and cook until it turns mushy, then add the sprouted beans and mix well. Add about 3 cups of water, cover, and simmer for 10–15 minutes or until mung sprouts are tender. Stir in the coriander and serve with roti flatbreads or rice.

Ful Medames

When Edward Lear was in Egypt in January 1854 he wrote to his sister Ann, 'The broad-bean fields are a great pleasure to me now; they are all in full bloom;—the Arab name for beans is Fool,-& at first the sailors used to puzzle me very much when they pointed to the fields & said—"fool! fool!"' *Fūl,* or ful medames, is a staple food in Sudan and Egypt, often served at breakfast but may be eaten at any time. It is usually a simple dish of stewed fava beans with olive oil and cumin, although with limitless variations. When I was last in Egypt, several restaurants served the sweetest mini lemons, halved and wrapped in muslin, with your fūl so you could squeeze the juice into your beans without getting the pips.

SERVES 4–6

Ingredients

- 2 × 400 g (14 oz) cans fava beans
- 1 medium onion
- 2 cloves garlic, crushed
- 4 tbsp olive oil
- 2 tsp cumin
- ½ tsp chilli powder
- 2 large tomatoes, chopped
- 2 tbsp tahini
- Juice of 1 lemon

Drain the beans and warm over a medium heat with about half a cup of water. Using a potato masher or the back of a fork, roughly mash the beans with 2 tablespoons of the oil, the tahini, and lemon juice.

Fry the onion and garlic in a separate pot with the remaining oil over medium heat for 5 minutes, then add the cumin, chilli, and tomatoes. Add the beans and cook over a low heat for 15–20 minutes—you are aiming for a fairly chunky, soft purée. Add extra water if it seems too thick. Serve with warm pita bread.

Broad Beans in Lemon Sauce

Serves 4

Ingredients

500 g (1 lb) fresh or frozen broad beans
25 g (2 tbsp) unsalted butter
2 tbsp flour
250 ml (8 fl oz) stock
Juice of 1 lemon
2 egg yolks
Black pepper, to taste

Boil the broad beans for around 5 minutes until just tender, drain, and set aside. Melt half the butter, add the flour, and stir well. Gradually add the stock and allow to boil for a few minutes. Add the pepper then stir in the rest of the butter, the lemon juice, and egg yolks. Stir in the beans and serve.

Petits Pois à la Française

Eliza Acton introduced the English to the delights of buttery, braised peas with lettuce way back in 1845 and it remains a popular dish, although the English do seem inclined to add bacon and not bother with the lettuce.

Serves 4

Ingredients

400 g (14 oz) fresh or frozen garden peas, defrosted and drained
8 small shallots
1 cos-type lettuce, separated into leaves
75 g (5 tbsp) butter
75 ml (3 fl oz) white wine
Small handful of fresh mint leaves
½ tsp honey (it won't actually keep them on your knife, but it does bring out the natural sweetness of the peas)

Peel, trim, and cut the shallots in half. Use half the butter to coat the bottom of a warm medium-sized saucepan then line with lettuce leaves. Fill with the peas, shallots, and some mint leaves and dot with the rest of the butter. Drizzle with honey and pour in the wine, then top with another layer of lettuce leaves. Set the pan over a gentle heat and simmer slowly for 30 minutes, shaking the pan occasionally. Transfer the vegetables to a warm serving dish, turn up the heat, and reduce the cooking liquid to a thick sauce. Pour over the peas and scatter with a little more mint.

Peas à l'Alexandra

Agnes Bertha Marshall (1852–1905) was the celebrity chef of her time. Renowned for popularising ice cream as a dessert, she was interested in all aspects of food. This recipe is adapted from her 1891 *Mrs. A.B. Marshall's Larger Cookery Book of Extra Recipes.* She recommends serving the peas in the centre of a border of red Pilau rice 'for a luncheon or second-course dish in the place of game or poultry.'

Serves 4

Ingredients

- 500 g (4 cups) fresh or frozen garden peas, defrosted and drained
- 4 large tomatoes
- 2 shallots, finely chopped
- 50 g (3.5 tbsp) butter
- 50 g (2 oz) streaky bacon, diced
- Small handful of fresh mint leaves
- 25 g (3 heaping tbsp) plain flour
- 75 ml (2.5 fl oz) double cream

Rub the pulp of the tomatoes through a sieve and add to a saucepan with the peas, butter, shallots, mint, and bacon. Simmer gently for about 15–20 minutes, occasionally shaking them about. Stir the flour into the cream then add to the peas and allow to boil for a few minutes, then serve.

Mushy Peas

Also known affectionately as 'Yorkshire caviar,' mushy peas are an ideal comfort food, and of course the traditional accompaniment to fish and chips. If you are not a traditionalist and like your meals with a pop of colour, try omitting the baking soda and add around ¼ teaspoon of matcha, a finely-powdered Japanese green tea from shade-grown tea leaves. It has a bright green colour and adds a grassy, umami flavour.

Serves 6–8

Ingredients

- 500 g (1 lb) dried marrowfat peas
- 1 tsp bicarbonate of soda
- 25 g (2 tbsp) butter, cubed
- Handful of fresh mint leaves, finely chopped
- Juice of 1 lemon

Dissolve the baking soda in a cup of boiling water. Place the dried marrowfat peas in a bowl and pour the water over them, topping up with more water so they are thoroughly covered. Give the peas a stir, then leave them to soak for 8 hours or overnight.

Drain and rinse the peas and place them in a saucepan with about 1500 ml (6 cups) of water. Bring to a boil, then reduce the heat, cover, and simmer for about 30 minutes until soft and mushy. Stir in the butter, mint, and lemon juice and serve.

Ethiopian Spiced Lentils

I once spent 8 hours in the Addis Ababa airport. It was late at night and I did not want to eat but a friendly waiter at the airport's main restaurant kindly talked me through the menu, explaining what was in every dish. His go-to recommendation for the end of a long day was a bowl of spiced lentils known as *misir wat*. A staple ingredient in the cuisine of Ethiopia and Eritrea is *niter kibbeh*, a clarified butter. It differs from ghee in that it is spiced and thus adds a lot of flavour and richness to recipes. For a truly authentic niter kibbeh you need besobela (Ethiopian sacred basil) and kosseret, which is in the verbena family. These are difficult to find outside of Ethiopia, but for an inauthentic lentil dish you can use butter or ghee and add some extra cardamom to the recipe. Berbere is a famously, fiery Ethiopian spice blend. You can buy it from specialist suppliers or make your own.

Ingredients

For the berbere

- 2 tsp coriander seeds
- 1 tsp cumin seeds
- ½ tsp fenugreek seeds
- 1 tsp black peppercorns
- Seeds from 4 green cardamom pods
- 4 cloves
- 5 dried red chilli peppers
- 3 tbsp sweet paprika
- 1 tsp turmeric
- 1 tsp salt
- ½ tsp ground ginger
- ¼ tsp nutmeg
- ¼ tsp cinnamon

Toast the whole spices and chillies in a heavy pan for about 3 minutes, shaking the pan regularly to prevent them from scorching. Allow to cool and then grind in a mortar and pestle or spice grinder. Mix the ground spices and salt together.

For the misir wat

- 50 g (3.5 tbsp) butter, ghee, or niter kibbeh
- 1 large onion, finely diced
- 3 cloves garlic, finely minced
- 1 large tomato, chopped
- 3 tbsp tomato paste
- 2 tbsp berbere
- 200 g (1 cup) red lentils, rinsed
- 600 ml (2½ cups) stock

Melt the ghee/niter kibbeh in a medium saucepan over medium heat. Add the onion and cook for 8–10 minutes until golden brown. Add the garlic, tomato, tomato paste, and 1 tablespoon of the berbere and cook for 5–7 minutes. Pour in the stock and lentils, bring it to a boil, then reduce the heat, cover, and simmer for 30–40 minutes, stirring occasionally, until the lentils are soft. This is traditionally served with Ethiopian injera, a teff sourdough flatbread.

Warm French Bean Salad

You can of course serve this cold but the flavour of the beans is more pronounced when warm.

Serves 4

Ingredients

- 500 g (1 lb) green beans, rinsed
- 2 shallots, finely diced
- 2 cloves garlic, crushed
- 2 tbsp red wine vinegar
- Juice of ½ lemon
- 2 tbsp vegetable oil
- 2 tsp whole grain mustard
- Black pepper, to taste

Combine the shallots, garlic, vinegar, lemon juice, and pepper in a large bowl and whisk in the mustard and oil. Set this aside. Steam or boil the green beans for 2–3 minutes until just tender. Drain and add into the bowl with the vinaigrette, stir, then allow them to marinate for 5 minutes or so before serving.

Black Bean Salad

Serves 4

Ingredients

- 1 × 400 g (14 oz or 3 cups) canned or precooked black (turtle) beans, drained and rinsed (or use any mixed beans)
- Zest and juice of 1 lime
- ½ tsp cumin
- 2 cloves garlic, minced
- 2 tbsp walnut, avocado, or olive oil
- 2 avocados or 2 handfuls boiled edamame beans or walnuts
- 1 large tomato, diced
- 12 cherry tomatoes, halved
- 3 spring onions, finely sliced
- Black pepper to taste

Whisk together the lime juice and zest, cumin, garlic, oil, and pepper. In a large bowl, combine the remaining ingredients. Pour the dressing on top and toss to combine.

Green Pea Guacamole

Avocados are wonderful, but for those of us who cannot grow them in our gardens, they are expensive and hardly sustainable eating, involving as they do many 'food miles' of transport. This simple guacamole substitute uses fresh or frozen garden peas as a tasty and nutritious alternative to pile on some toasted sourdough bread. The yogurt adds the silky smoothness normally provided by the avocado but can be omitted if you have to avoid dairy foods.

Serves 4

Ingredients

- 250 g (2 cups) fresh or frozen green peas, boiled
- 2 tbsp Greek yogurt
- 1 tsp crushed garlic
- 2 tbsp fresh lime juice
- ½ tsp ground cumin
- 1 large tomato, chopped
- 4 spring onions, chopped
- ½ cup chopped fresh coriander (cilantro)
- ½ tsp harissa paste

Blend the peas, garlic, lime juice, and cumin with a hand blender or food processor until smooth. Stir in the tomato, onions, coriander, yogurt, and harissa. Cover and refrigerate for half an hour or so, to allow the flavours to blend and mellow.

Black Bean Chocolate Mousse

SERVES 4–6

Ingredients

- 1 × 400 g (14 oz) can black or kidney beans, drained and rinsed
- 50 g (1½ oz) dried stoned dates
- 8 tbsp maple syrup
- 4 tbsp cocoa powder
- 4 tbsp single cream
- Grated zest and juice of 1 orange

Soak the dates with the zest and orange juice for a couple of hours or overnight. Blend the beans, dates, syrup, and cocoa together until smooth using a hand blender or food processor. Stir in the cream, then spoon the mixture into ramekins or espresso cups and chill until required. If you want to make a dairy-free/vegan version, replace the cream with 2 tablespoons of melted coconut oil.

Habichuelas Con Dulce

Habichuelas con dulce is a sweet, creamy Dominican dessert made with beans, coconut milk, sweet potatoes, and spices. It is traditionally served during Lent with biscuits or a toasted cassava flatbread.

SERVES 4

Ingredients

- 200 g (1½ cups) precooked/canned red kidney beans, rinsed and drained
- 250 ml (1 cup) coconut milk
- 250 ml (1 cup) evaporated milk
- 100 g (½ cup) sugar
- 100 g (4 oz) sweet potato, diced
- 100 g (½ cup) raisins
- 1 tsp vanilla extract
- 1 cinnamon stick
- ½ tsp ground cloves

Blend the beans with a cup of water. Sieve to get rid of the skins. Pour the sieved beans, coconut, and evaporated milk, sugar, vanilla, cinnamon, cloves, and sweet potatoes into a saucepan. Simmer over a low heat for about 20 minutes until the sweet potato is soft, stirring regularly to avoid sticking. Add the raisins and simmer for another 10 minutes. Turn off the heat and remove the cinnamon stick. Allow to cool, then chill before serving.

Noah's Pudding

The traditional dessert of Turkey and Armenia known as *ashure*, *trigo koço*, or Noah's pudding gets its common name from its reputed origin as a celebratory dish made by Noah's family when his biblical ark came to rest on Mount Ararat. They supposedly put all their remaining food supplies, a mixture of grains, pulses, and dried fruits into a pudding which they ate while waiting for the waters to recede.

Serves 8

Ingredients

- 100 g (½ cup) pearl barley
- 100 g (½ cup) pudding rice
- 200 g (8 oz or 1½ cups) precooked/canned white beans, rinsed and drained
- 200 g (8 oz or 1½ cups) precooked/canned chickpeas, rinsed and drained
- 1000 ml (4 cups) water
- 8 dried apricots, chopped
- 4 dried figs, chopped
- 100 g (½ cup) raisins
- Juice and grated zest of 1 small orange
- Grated zest of 1 lemon
- 1 tsp ground cinnamon
- 1 tsp ground nutmeg
- Seeds from 2 cardamom pods, ground
- 100 g (½ cup) sugar
- 50 g (½ cup) ground almonds
- 50 g (½ cup) walnuts, roughly chopped
- 50 g (½ cup) pistachios, roughly chopped
- 1 pomegranate, seeded

Place the barley and rice in a large saucepan with the water and the lemon and orange zest. Bring to a boil, then reduce the heat, cover, and simmer for 45 minutes. Add the beans, dried fruits, and spices and simmer for another 15–20 minutes, adding more water or up to a cup of milk if it starts to dry out. Stir in the orange juice, ground almonds, and sugar. Pour into dessert cups and top with the nuts and pomegranate seeds.

Sri Lankan Pongal Pudding

Pongal is a Sri Lankan rice pudding which includes lentils as well as the rice. The sweetness traditionally comes from jaggery, lumps of cane sugar, but you can use honey or a dark brown or demerara sugar. If the milk overflows while cooking your pudding during the Pongal celebrations in January, it is taken as a sign of prosperity and omen for a successful harvest.

Serves 4

Ingredients

- 100 g (½ cup) basmati rice
- 100 g (½ cup) red lentils
- 400 ml (14 fl oz) tin coconut milk
- 100 g (½ cup) jaggery or brown sugar
- 1 tsp ground cardamom
- 50 g (¼ cup) raisins
- 50 g (½ cup) cashew nuts, toasted

Rinse the rice and lentils in cold water. Add to a saucepan with 250 ml (1 cup) water and bring to a boil. Stir in the coconut milk. Bring back to a boil and then reduce the heat to a gentle simmer. Cook for 20–25 minutes, stirring frequently, until the rice and lentils are tender. Add the sugar and cardamom and stir, then stir in the dried fruit and cashew nuts. Continue to cook for a further few minutes, then serve while it is still hot.

Danpatjuk

This Korean sweet red bean porridge is a comforting dessert made of boiled and mashed red beans. It is traditionally eaten around the time of the winter solstice. The red colour was thought to drive away evil spirits and prevent disease.

Serves 4

Ingredients

- 300 g (1½ cups) dried red adzuki beans
- 3 tbsp rice flour
- 3 tbsp sugar
- ½ tsp cinnamon

Rinse the red beans thoroughly and place them in a large saucepan. Cover them with water, bring to a boil, and cook for 10 minutes then drain and discard the water. Return the beans to the saucepan. Add 1500 ml (6 cups) water and bring them to a boil again. Cover and simmer the beans over a low heat for about an hour adding more water if necessary to keep the beans covered. They should be soft enough to be easily squeezed between your fingers. Remove the pot from the heat and use a hand blender to blend the beans to a smooth consistency. Add the cinnamon, rice flour, and sugar and simmer for 5 minutes. Ladle into serving bowls and top with chopped nuts or banana. It is best served warm.

Italian Chocolate Salami

Not the meat salami, but a salami-shaped rich chocolate dessert that is a sophisticated Italian take on chocolate refrigerator cake. Nigella Lawson does a particularly indulgent version which is heavy on cream, butter and eggs.

Ingredients

- 200 g (8 oz or 1½ cups) precooked/canned white beans, rinsed and drained
- 4 Medjoul dates, stones removed
- 200 g (8 oz) dark chocolate
- 200 g (1 cup) butter
- 200 g (8 oz) plain biscuits, roughly broken/crushed
- 50 g (½ cup) pistachios, roughly chopped
- Icing sugar to dust

Rinse and drain the cannellini beans then blend them with the dates in a food processor. Add the biscuits and mix together. Melt the chocolate and butter together in a saucepan over a low heat, then add the other ingredients and stir together. Pour the mixture onto a sheet of baking paper and roll it up into a sausage shape. Put it in the fridge for at least 4 hours to firm up, dust with icing sugar, and cut into slices.

Spring Green Ice Cream

The spring freshness of peas is a perfect basis for this vegan ice cream. Blanch the peas in order to retain their bright colour. If you do not have a jar of pistachio butter in the cupboard you can make your own by lightly toasting shelled and skinned pistachio nuts for a couple of minutes in a hot oven and then blitzing them in a blender or coffee grinder. There are plenty of videos available online to show you how it is done. Nadine Brown, writing for *Olive* magazine, adds vodka to her pea ice cream but a splash of gin may work too.

Ingredients

200 g (8 oz or 1¾ cups) fresh or frozen garden peas
400 ml (14 oz) can full fat coconut milk
200 g (1 cup) caster sugar
50 g (3 tbsp) pistachio butter
Grated zest and juice of 1 lime

Simmer the peas for 2 minutes then tip into a sieve, rinse with cold water, and drain. Put the coconut milk and sugar in a pan over a medium heat and simmer gently until the sugar has dissolved. Remove from the heat and leave to cool. Blend the peas together with the coconut milk mixture. Stir in the lime juice, zest, and pistachio butter. Chill until completely cold. Pour the mixture into a large plastic container and freeze for 1 hour. Remove from the freezer and whisk with an electric whisk to break up the ice crystals, then return to the freezer. Repeat this three times (or use an ice cream maker). Return to the freezer for a few more hours to freeze solid.

Clover Blossom Syrup

Clovers are invaluable in a wildlife garden, enriching the soil and attracting bumblebees and other nectar feeding insects. The leaves are edible with a mild pea-like flavour, although to be frank they are

FIG. 38. Clover syrup.

fairly chewy and indigestible even when cooked. The flowers have a rich, sweet scent and can be eaten scattered over salads or dried for herbal teas. They can also be used to make this clover blossom syrup which is a lovely viscous liquid that looks like bottled summer. It can be used as a cheap honey substitute or served drizzled over ice cream.

Ingredients

- 2 large mugfuls clover flowers
- 1000 ml (4 cups) water
- 1 kg (2.2 lb) sugar
- 1 small orange, chopped with the peel

Put the flowers and orange into a large pan with the water and bring to the boil. Turn off the heat, cover the pan, and leave to infuse overnight. Strain through muslin or a clean tea towel, squeezing out all the liquid. Return the liquid to the rinsed pan. (The flowers can go in the compost heap.) Add the sugar to the liquid then slowly bring to boil, stirring from time to time. Reduce the heat and simmer until the liquid has reduced to a thick syrup. Bottle into sterile jars. The sugar can start to crystallize fairly quickly but the syrup tastes so good it does not usually hang around long. Stirring in half a teaspoon (3–5 g) citric acid will help to preserve it for longer.

Baking with Beans

Eliza Acton's French-Bean Bread

Eliza Acton's *The English Bread-book* was published in 1857. Subtitled, 'for domestic use, adapted to families of every grade: containing the plainest and most minute instructions to the learner; practical receipts for many varieties of bread; with notices of the present system of adulteration, and its consequences; and of the improved baking processes and institutions established abroad,' it is available online courtesy of The Wellcome Collection. She warns that the dried seed of white French beans were not considered suitable for invalids but 'When quite fresh, it is less objectionable than after it is harvested for winter consumption.' However, 'for persons whose digestion is not extremely delicate' she thought that using the beans to replace a proportion of wheat flour took advantage of their nutritious properties without impacting the flavour and appearance of the bread.

MAKES 2 LOAVES

Ingredients

- 2 × 400 g (14 oz can or 6 cups) precooked haricot or other white beans
- 900 g (7.5 cups) bread flour
- 2 sachets (10 g) of active dry/instant yeast
- 20 g (3¼ tsp) salt
- *(optional: beaten egg/milk to glaze)*

Push the beans through a sieve to remove skins (although if you are of strong digestion, you could just blitz them to a puree with a blender). Combine the yeast, salt, and flour in a large bowl. Mix in 500 ml (2 cups) warm water and the beans, working the dough thoroughly until it no longer clings to the sides of the bowl. Add more flour if it feels too sticky. Cover the bowl with a tea towel and leave in a warm place to rise for 30 minutes. Knead dough for a few minutes then shape into rolls or two loaves and place on greased baking trays. Cover and allow to rise for another 30 minutes. Brush the loaf with egg wash or milk if desired and bake at 220°C (430°F) for 20–25 minutes, until golden brown and sounding hollow.

Savoury Chickpea Scones

These are lovely warm from the oven but unfortunately harden much faster than standard scones, so freeze any that are not going to be eaten the same day.

MAKES 8

Ingredients

- 240 g (2 cups) chickpea flour
- 1 tsp paprika
- 2 tsp baking powder
- 250 ml (1 cup) milk
- 75 ml (5½ tbsp) vegetable oil
- 2 eggs
- 2 tbsp tomato puree
- 50 g hard cheese, grated

Reserve a little egg and milk for egg wash and a small handful of the cheese. Mix all the ingredients together in a large bowl then knead lightly on a floured work surface. Roll gently into a circle and mark into 8 pieces or cut into 8 individual scones. Brush with the egg wash and sprinkle with remaining cheese. Bake at 220°C (430°F) for 20 minutes until golden brown.

Black Bean Brownies

Ingredients

1 × 400 g (14 oz or 3 cups) canned or precooked black or kidney beans, drained and rinsed
200 g (8 oz) dark chocolate
50 g (5 tbsp) cocoa powder
50 g (6½ tbsp) self-raising flour
½ tsp baking powder
4 eggs
100 g (½ cup) demerara sugar
100 g (½ cup) melted butter (or coconut or vegetable oil)
2 tsp vanilla extract

Melt the chocolate in a bain-marie (double-boiler) or in the microwave. Combine all the other ingredients until smooth, then stir in the chocolate. Pour into a greased and lined 20 cm (8″) square baking tray. Cook at 180°C (350°F) for 15–20 minutes, until set but still a little squidgy; they will firm up on cooling.

Black Bean Cake

While you have got the beans out, do try this sweet, fudgy chocolate cake. I like it topped with a chocolate ganache but you can use a buttercream frosting if you prefer.

Ingredients

1 × 400 g (14 oz or 3 cups) canned or precooked black or kidney beans, drained and rinsed
150 g (⅔ cup) demerara sugar
4 eggs
100 g (½ cup) melted butter (or coconut or vegetable oil)
1 tsp vanilla extract
25 g (2½ tbsp) cocoa
1 tsp baking powder
150 g (6 tbsp) apricot jam

For the ganache

100 g (4 oz) dark chocolate
100 ml (4 oz) double cream

Blend the beans to a smooth puree then mix with the sugar, eggs, butter, vanilla, baking powder, and cocoa. Pour into a lined 20 cm (8″) cake tin and bake for around 30 minutes at 180°C (350°F). Allow to cool, then split horizontally and sandwich together with most of the jam. Add a little hot water to the remaining jam, stir it together, and then brush it on the top and sides of the cake.

Warm the chocolate and cream in a small pan, stirring until combined. Tip over the cake and smooth with a warm palette knife.

Lemon Bean Cake

There is no added wheat flour in this recipe, meaning that this cake is gluten-free, so long as you use a gluten-free baking powder. It is delicious served with authentic Greek yogurt.

Serves 8

Ingredients

- 2 × 400 g (14 oz can or 6 cups) precooked cannelloni or other white beans
- 200 g (1 cup) sugar
- 1 tsp vanilla essence
- 4 eggs
- 100 g (1 cup) ground almonds
- 2 tsp baking powder
- 100 g (½ cup) melted butter or coconut oil

For lemon syrup

- Juice and grated zest of 1 lemon
- 50 g (½ cup) icing sugar

Grease and line a 20 cm (8″) springform cake tin. Blend the drained beans with the sugar and vanilla until smooth. Add the eggs, almonds, baking powder, and melted butter and mix thoroughly. Pour into the prepared tin and bake at 180°C (350°F) for 30–40 minutes, until golden brown on top and firm to the touch. Combine the icing sugar, lemon juice, and zest and heat in a microwave or a small pan until the sugar has dissolved. Make several holes in the cake with a skewer and then pour the syrup over the cake.

Lupin and Almond Clementine Cake

This lovely moist cake is based on Nigella Lawson's clementine cake, which she reports is based on one made by Claudia Roden. If you do not have lupin flour, you can use chickpea flour.

Serves 8

Ingredients

- 4 clementines, unpeeled
- 100 g (1 cup) almond flour
- 100 g (1 cup) lupin flour
- 200 g (1 cup) sugar
- 2 tsp baking powder
- ½ tsp ground cardamon
- 4 large eggs
- 150 ml (⅔ cup) natural Greek yogurt or sour cream

Simmer the clementines in a large pan of water for about an hour. Drain and allow to cool. Grease and line a 20 cm (8″) springform pan with parchment paper. Slice the clementines in half and flick out the seeds, then blitz to a puree with a blender. Beat the eggs with the flour, sugar, almonds, cardamon, and baking powder, then mix in the pulped oranges and pour into the tin. Bake at 180°C (350°F) for 50–60 minutes. Allow to cool then remove from the tin.

Peanut Butter Flapjacks

Serves 16

Ingredients

- 400 g (14 oz) porridge/rolled oats
- 250 g (1 cup + 2 tbsp) butter
- 150 g (⅔ cup) crunchy peanut butter
- 150 g (¾ cup) demerara sugar
- 150 g (6 tbsp) golden syrup

Melt the butter, peanut butter, golden syrup, and sugar together in a large pan on a medium heat. Stir in the oats and mix thoroughly. Pour into a lined 20 cm (8″) square baking tin and spread it evenly into all four corners. (If you prefer your flapjack thin and brittle use a Swiss roll tin.) With the back of a spoon or silicone spatula, press the flapjack mixture down. Bake in the oven for 20 minutes at 180°C (350°F) or until the edges have turned golden brown. Allow to cool and then cut into slices.

Hilbeh

Fenugreek has an interesting bittersweet flavour and is used in Palestine and across the Levant to make this sweet and sticky yeasted cake with semolina and olive oil. The fenugreek seeds are boiled before being used to reduce bitterness.

Ingredients

4 tbsp fenugreek seeds
500 g (1 lb) fine semolina
250 g (2 cups) all purpose flour
½ tsp ground cinnamon
½ tsp ground cardamon
60 ml (4 tbsp) olive oil
100 g (½ cup) butter, melted
1 tsp sugar
1 sachet (5 g) of active dry/instant yeast

For the syrup

Juice and grated zest of 1 lemon
100 g (½ cup) sugar
2 tsp orange blossom water, if available
250 ml (1 cup) water

Boil the seeds in 750 ml (6 cups) of water, reduce the heat, and simmer for 20 minutes. Drain the cooked fenugreek seeds and reserve the water. Allow the water to cool to a hand-hot temperature. Put 120 ml (½ cup) of the water in a bowl and stir in the sugar and yeast. Set aside to froth.

Mix the drained seeds, semolina, flour, cardamom, and cinnamon in a large bowl and pour in the olive oil and butter. Add the yeast mixture and gently knead the dough together. Add extra fenugreek water if needed to make a soft pliable dough. Spread the dough onto a lightly greased 23 × 30 cm (9 × 12″) baking tin, pressing the dough down evenly. Score into diamond shaped pieces. Set aside in a warm place for 15–30 minutes to rise. Bake at 180°C (350°F) for about 15–20 minutes or until golden brown. Meanwhile, make the sugar syrup by bringing the water, lemon juice, orange blossom water, and sugar to the boil in a small pan. Once the cake is out of the oven, pour the syrup over and leave to cool. Store in an airtight tin.

Savoury Snacks

Roasted Broad Beans

Traditional deep-fried *habas fritas* are Spanish crunchy fried broad beans, often served as a salted snack as part of a tapas platter. This version is cooked in the oven and uses herbs to enhance the flavours. You can use canned beans but they tend to be smaller and shrivel up quite a bit during roasting. Butter beans work well.

Ingredients

- 300 g (2 cups) fresh or frozen broad beans or dried split fava beans, pre-cooked.
- 1 tbsp olive oil
- 1 tsp dried rosemary
- 1 tsp dried thyme
- ½ tsp salt

Grind the rosemary and thyme in a mortar and pestle. Drain the beans and remove the skins by gently squeezing them on the rounded edge so the inner part of the bean pops out. If the beans are young and freshly picked, omit this stage. You can keep older beans in the skins (they are a good source of fibre), but they can be quite chewy. Spread the beans out on a baking sheet, drizzle with oil, and sprinkle with salt and ground herbs. Give them a good stir with your hands to split the seed leaves apart and ensure they are evenly covered with oil. Roast at 180°C (350°F) for about 40 minutes, stirring them halfway, until crispy.

Roasted Chickpea Mix

This makes a good sustaining trail mix to take on days out in the countryside.

Serves 4 (or one long-distance hiker)

Ingredients

- 150 g (6 oz or 1 cup) canned chickpeas rinsed, drain and pat dry
- 1 tbsp olive oil
- 1 tsp paprika
- 1 tsp garlic powder
- 50 g (½ cup) roasted almonds
- 50 g (½ cup) roasted cashews
- 25 g (¼ cup) sunflower seeds
- 1 tbsp chia seed
- Pinch of salt

On a baking tray, toss the chickpeas with the olive oil, salt, paprika, and garlic powder until evenly coated. Spread the chickpeas in a single layer and bake at 180°C (350°F) for 15–20 minutes, or until crispy. Remove from the oven and allow the chickpeas to cool completely. If you have bought raw rather than roasted nuts, they will be best roasted on a separate tray to the chickpeas because they can cook quicker and are unpleasant if overdone. In a large bowl, add the roasted almonds, cashews, sunflower, and chia seeds. Add the roasted chickpeas and mix well.

Falafel

Falafel are deep-fried patties made of fava beans or chickpeas combined with herbs and spices. They originate in the Middle East where they are a popular street food. This recipe is based on one from the Egyptian writer Magda Mehdawy but there are infinite variations. Dried split fava beans (or crushed dry broad beans) are available from specialist suppliers but use chickpeas or green split peas if you cannot find them. Green peas do give a lovely colour to the falafel.

MAKES 16

Ingredients

- 500 g (1 lb) dried split fava beans or fava bean chips, soaked overnight
- 1 onion
- 1 leek
- Handful of fresh coriander (cilantro)
- Handful of fresh mint leaves
- 1 red chilli pepper
- Zest of 1 lemon
- ½ tsp ground black pepper
- 1 tsp cayenne pepper
- 2 tsp ground cumin
- ½ tsp cinnamon
- 1 egg, beaten
- 1 tbsp milk
- Sesame seeds
- Vegetable oil for deep frying

FIG. 39. Falafel with a cream cheese dip.

Roughly chop the onion, leek, herbs, and chilli. Mix with the beans, spices, and lemon zest, and blend with a hand blender or in a food processor until reasonably smooth. Stir in about half of the egg. Roll tablespoons of the mixture into balls then flatten slightly and refrigerate for 30 minutes. Add the milk to the rest of the egg. Dip the patties into the egg-milk wash then sprinkle with sesame seeds. Deep fry in hot oil until golden. This can be served hot and fresh or cold, perhaps in a picnic or packed lunch.

Chickpea Flatbreads

Known in the Mediterranean region as *farinata di ceci* or *socca*, these pancake-like breads are made from chickpea flour (garbanzo bean flour) and are gluten free. In the French city of Nice they are cooked on large copper pans in a wood-fired oven, but a pizza pan or heavy frying pan will do.

Serves 4

Ingredients

- 100 g (1 cup) chickpea flour
- 2 tbsp olive oil
- 1 tsp dried thyme

Put ½ tablespoon oil in your cooking pan. Whisk the flour with 250 ml (1 cup) water, the rest of the oil, and the thyme in a medium bowl until smooth. Let the batter rest for 30 minutes to give the flour time to absorb the water. Heat your pan then pour in the batter. You can either bake this griddle cake in a hot oven or treat it as a pancake and cook it on the hob, finishing it under a hot grill. Do not overcook—the inside should still be moist and creamy. Socca is definitely best eaten hot from the oven.

Karantika

If you have bought chickpea flour to make the Chickpea Flatbreads, then do use the leftovers to try this Algerian chickpea pie. More quiche-like than pie, the name karantika (garantita) comes from the Spanish word *caliente*, meaning 'hot.' This is a simple street food that can be eaten on its own as a snack, as a side dish, or as a sandwich filling. The dish is said to have originated when the Spanish invaded

Oran in western Algeria in 1509. Some versions make a simpler batter without the eggs.

Serves 4

Ingredients

- 200 g (2 cups) chickpea flour
- 2 eggs
- 75 ml (5 tbsp) vegetable oil
- 1000 ml (4 cups) water
- ¼ tsp black pepper
- 2 tsp baking powder
- 1 tbsp cumin powder
- Harissa, to serve

Whisk the chickpea flour, baking powder, eggs, oil, salt, pepper, cumin, and water together in a large bowl. Allow to stand for 30 minutes, stir, and then pour into a greased ceramic baking dish, approximately 23 cm (9″) square. Bake in a 200°C (400°F) preheated oven for about 30 minutes until golden brown but still wobbly. Serve hot with French bread and harissa paste.

Chickpea Tortillas

You can use besan or gram flour, which is made from brown desi chickpeas, for these tortillas. Besan is less absorbent than the chickpea flour made from white garbanzo beans, so less water is needed. Arrowroot starch, usually made from the rhizome of the American plant *Maranta arundinacea*, helps the tortillas retain flexibility so you can use them as wraps.

Serves 3

Ingredients

- 150 g (1½ cups) chickpea flour
- 50 g (½ cup) arrowroot starch
- 1 egg
- 1 tsp baking powder
- Pinch chilli flakes or 1 tsp paprika
- 500 ml (2 cups) water
- 2 tbsp vegetable oil

Combine the flour, starch, egg, chilli, and baking powder in a bowl. Add the water. Beat thoroughly into a batter. Allow to stand for half an hour to thicken a bit. Heat a generous splash of oil in a pancake griddle or frying pan over medium heat. Add ⅓ of the batter. Cook gently, pushing the edges with a spatula to check when it is ready to flip over. You should be able to move the tortilla without it sticking to the pan and the top should be thickening a little. Flip and cook the other side until it can be slid round without sticking. Put aside on a warm plate while cooking another two tortillas, then serve as tacos or wraps.

Mini Baked Bean Muffins

Makes 24

Ingredients

- 200 g (7 oz) canned baked beans
- 15 g (1 tbsp) butter
- 1 tsp olive oil
- 3 spring onions, finely sliced
- ¼ small red bell pepper, finely diced
- 180 g (1½ cups) self-rising flour
- 120 ml (½ cup) milk
- 1 tsp paprika
- 1 egg, beaten
- 1 courgette, grated
- 50 g (3 tbsp) hard cheese, grated

Grease a mini muffin tin with oil or line with paper cases. Heat the oil in a small pan over medium heat, add the spring onion and pepper and cook for a couple of minutes until softened. Remove from heat and drain on absorbent paper. Melt the butter and mix in a bowl with the milk, egg, and flour. Fold in the cooked onions and pepper, grated courgette, baked beans, and cheese.

Spoon into the muffin cases and bake at 180°C (350°F) for 12–15 minutes until cooked through and golden. Remove muffins to a wire rack to cool.

Moi Moi

Moi moi or moin moin, is a Nigerian steamed, savoury bean pudding made from blended black-eye beans, peppers, onions, and spices. The beans are sometimes sold pre-skinned but you could use split yellow peas. Traditionally, the moi moi paste is wrapped in banana leaves before steaming but if you do not grow banana plants, then you can steam individual portions in ramekins.

Makes 6

Ingredients

- 400 g (2 cups) dried black-eye beans
- 1 red onion
- 2 large tomatoes
- 1 red bell pepper
- 1 hot chilli pepper
- 2 tbsp vegetable oil
- 4 tbsp stock

Rinse the beans, then boil for 10 minutes and allow to cool in the water. Rub them between your hands to peel and discard the skins. Blend the beans, onions, peppers, and tomatoes with a hand blender or in a food processor with a little stock to form a thick batter. Stir in the vegetable oil then pour into ramekins. Stand these on a roasting tin of hot water and steam in a hot oven at around 200°C (400°F) for approximately 2 hours, until they are firm and start to pull away from the sides of the dish.

Sweet Snacks

Black Bean Fudge

Even if you have tried unsuccessfully every other way of getting the family to eat beans, this recipe for bean fudge may actually work. This fudge has a wonderful melt-in-your-mouth texture and it would require a highly-refined palate to detect the flavour of the black beans.

Ingredients

- 200 g (8 oz) dark chocolate
- 200 g (8 oz or 1½ cups) canned or precooked black beans, drained and rinsed
- 2 tbsp maple syrup
- 1 tsp pure vanilla extract

Line a 20 cm (8″) square pan with parchment paper. Use a hand blender or processor to blend the beans with the syrup and vanilla until smooth. Melt the chocolate in a bain-marie or in the microwave and stir into the bean mixture. Transfer to the prepared pan using a flat spatula or the back of a spoon to spread it evenly. Chill until set then cut into about 16 servings.

Easy Peanut Fudge

Get the children making this. Once set it is perfect for packing up to take on a picnic or for those 'Are we nearly there yet?' moments in the car.

Ingredients

200 g (⅞ cup) butter
200 g (¾ cup) smooth peanut butter (or crunchy if you prefer)
1 tsp vanilla extract
300 g (3 cups) icing sugar

Line a 20 cm (8″) square tin with parchment paper. Melt the butter, peanut butter, and vanilla extract together in a saucepan over a low heat or in the microwave in a ceramic/glass bowl for around 90 seconds. Stir to combine. Add the icing sugar, a cup or so at a time, stirring well to combine thoroughly. Transfer the fudge mixture to the pan and press until smooth. Chill for around 4 hours before cutting into squares. If you are feeling particularly indulgent you can dip the squares in melted chocolate and set aside on a fresh piece of parchment to firm up. Store in an airtight container in the fridge for up to two weeks.

Peanut Butter Cookies

Makes 8–10

Ingredients

1 ripe banana
75 g (1 cup) rolled oats
125 g (½ cup) peanut butter
1 tbsp golden or maple syrup
10 g (1 tbsp) cocoa powder
1 tbsp vanilla extract
2–3 tbsp milk

Mash the banana and then add in the other ingredients, stirring to form a thick cookie dough. Add a splash more milk if it seems dry, or shake in more oats if it is too wet. Put heaped tablespoons of the dough onto a greased baking tray and flatten slightly with a fork. Bake at 180°C (350°F) for 12–15 minutes until the edges are lightly golden. Transfer to a wire cooling rack and allow to cool completely before transferring to an airtight tin.

Sweet Lentil Cookies

Use peanut butter instead of the almond butter if you prefer and you can substitute maple syrup for the golden syrup.

Makes 16

Ingredients

100 g (½ cup) red lentils, rinsed
2 tbsp orange juice
125 g (½ cup) almond butter
100 g (4 tbsp) golden syrup
75 g (1 cup) rolled oats
1 egg
1 tsp vanilla extract
1 tsp baking powder
50 g (¼ cup) chocolate chips

Put the red lentils in a small saucepan with a 250 ml (1 cup) of water. Bring to a boil, then reduce the heat and simmer for 15–20 minutes, or until all of the water has been absorbed. Allow to cool then puree the cooked lentils with the orange juice and vanilla until smooth.

In a large bowl, whisk together the nut butter, egg, and syrup. Then stir in the lentils. Add the oats, baking powder, and chocolate chips and stir until combined. Put heaped tablespoons of the dough onto a greased baking tray and flatten slightly with a fork. Bake at 180°C (350°F) for 20–25 minutes until firm and the edges are lightly golden. Transfer to a wire cooling rack and allow to cool completely before transferring to an airtight tin.

Black Bean Truffles

Makes 16

Ingredients

200 g (8 oz) black beans, canned or precooked
200 g (8 oz) dried dates
200 g (¾ cup) almond butter (or other nut butter)
50 g (5 tbsp) cocoa powder
50 ml (3½ tbsp) orange juice
Chocolate vermicelli or desiccated coconut, to roll the truffles

Place the dates in a saucepan with the orange juice and bring to boil. Turn off the heat and leave to soak for an hour. Blend the dates with the beans, nut butter, and cocoa powder using a hand blender or food processor until you have a firm paste. With your hands, roll into balls and then coat the truffles in vermicelli or coconut. Store in the refrigerator in an airtight container.

Besan Ladoo

This traditional Indian sweet, made from gram flour (besan), sugar, and ghee is commonly made at homes during Diwali and other special occasions.

It is delicately flavoured with cardamom. Slow toasting of the gram flour in ghee ensures it becomes aromatic and turns a rich golden-brown.

Ingredients

- 250 g (2 cups) gram flour
- 100 g (½ cup) ghee or butter
- 125 g (1¼ cups) icing sugar
- 2 tbsp ground almonds
- ½ tsp ground cardamom
- 1 tbsp flaked almonds, for decoration

Heat ghee in a deep non-stick pan, add the flour and cook on a medium heat for approximately 10 minutes. Set aside to cool. Add the sugar, almonds, and cardamom and mix well. Take tablespoon-sized portions of the mixture and shape it into balls with your hands. Garnish with almond slivers and store in an air-tight container.

Aquafaba Meringues

Chickpeas, like other legume seeds, contain albumins and globulins, which are the same proteins found in eggs. They are also rich in saponins, organic chemicals that act like soaps, dissolving in both fat and water. This means that they can form stable foams. Aquafaba simply means bean water and is the term used to describe the water that is drained from cooked pulses, but most commonly chickpeas. The liquid drained from canned chickpeas has a viscosity similar to that of egg whites and works well. The presence of albumins, globulins, and saponins in the liquid means that, when agitated, it can be used for culinary foams, including egg-less meringues. Adding cream of tartar helps to stabilise the meringue.

Ingredients

- 100 ml (½ cup) aquafaba (chickpea water from a 400 g can of chickpeas)
- ¼ tsp cream of tartar
- 200 g (1 cup) caster sugar

Whisk the aquafaba with the cream of tartar in a stand mixer at high speed for at least 15–20 minutes until stiff white peaks have formed. With the mixer running, add the sugar a few tablespoons at a time, whisking well after each addition. When the mixture is thick and glossy spoon it onto lined baking sheets. Bake at 120°C (250°F) for 60 minutes, then switch the oven off but leave the meringues inside for another hour without opening the door. If you are not going to eat them the same day, they can be kept in an airtight container in the fridge for 5 days.

Apple and Black Bean Jam

This versatile jam can be eaten simply on crusty bread or toast. You can also try adding spoonfuls of it to stir fries and pork casseroles.

MAKES ABOUT 4 × 450 G JARS

Ingredients

- 2 large cooking apples, peeled and roughly chopped
- 250 g (10 oz or 2 cups) canned or precooked black beans, drained, rinsed, and mashed
- 1000 ml (4 cups) water
- 400 g (2 cups) white sugar
- 125 ml (½ cup) lemon juice

Mix mashed beans with water and bring to a boil. Remove from heat, add sugar and lemon juice, then stir until sugar is dissolved. Return to the heat and boil until a setting point is reached, removing any scum as it forms. To determine if the jam has set, use a spoon to transfer some of the boiling preserve from the pan to a saucer which has been chilled in a fridge. Allow the preserve to cool and then push it gently with your forefinger. If the preserve wrinkles, it has reached its setting point. Fill into clean jars.

DRINKS

Homemade Pea Milk

For vegans and anyone with a dairy allergy, this is a useful plant-based milk substitute with a naturally creamy texture due to the sunflower oil, that acts as an emulsifier, keeping it from splitting in coffee.

Ingredients

- 250 g (1 cup) dry yellow split peas
- 2 tbsp sunflower oil
- ½ tsp vanilla extract
- Pinch of salt

Put the peas in a bowl with 750 ml (3 cups) of water. Cover and leave to soak for 8 hours or overnight. Drain and rinse the peas, then put them in a saucepan along with 750 ml (3 cups) of fresh water. Bring to a boil, then reduce the heat and simmer with the lid on for 45 minutes to an hour, or until the peas are soft. Drain and blend with 750 ml (3 cups) of fresh water, the oil, vanilla extract, and salt until smooth. Hang a muslin cloth or jelly bag over a large bowl and pour the pea milk into the bag. Squeeze so the pea milk drains through and the pulp remains inside. Transfer the liquid to a bottle with an air-tight lid and place in the fridge. The pea milk can be kept for up to 4 days in a refrigerator.

Peanut Butter and Banana Smoothie

This smoothie has no added sugar as it is naturally sweetened with bananas. You can pre-freeze the banana by peeling them, then cutting them into large chunks and dipping in lemon juice to reduce browning, before flash freezing on a baking sheet. Once solid, transfer chunks to a freezer bag or airtight container and store them until needed.

Serves 2

Ingredients

- 250 ml (1 cup) milk
- 1 large banana, chopped and frozen
- 2 tbsp smooth peanut butter

Blend ingredients together and divide between two glasses. Add two tablespoons of cocoa powder if you prefer a chocolatey taste.

Chocolate Bean Smoothie

Serves 2

Ingredients

- 100 g (4 oz or ½ cup) canned or precooked black beans, drained and rinsed
- 150 ml (⅔ cup) natural Greek yogurt
- 250 ml (1 cup) milk
- 1 banana, fresh or frozen
- 4 pitted dates
- 2 tbsp cocoa powder
- ¼ tsp peppermint extract, optional
- Some mint leaves and cocoa nibs, for decoration

Blend ingredients together and divide between two glasses.

Green Pea Syrup

This pretty syrup can be served diluted with lemonade or elderflower cordial or used as a basis for alcoholic cocktails. Skewer a few peas on a cocktail stick with a mint leaf to dress the glass.

Ingredients

- 400 g (8 oz or 3½ cups) fresh or frozen young garden peas
- 60 g (6 tbsp) light honey or clover or agave syrup
- Handful of fresh mint leaves, washed
- 125 ml (½ cup) water

Fig. 40. *Two Angels with a Peapod* engraving (1533) by German artist Master HL (active ca. 1511–33), The Metropolitan Museum of Art, New York, object no. 29.44.26.

Bring the peas to the boil in a pan of water, then drain and rinse with cold water.

Blend the peas with the mint leaves and pass through a fine sieve. Then stir in the honey or syrup and the ½ cup of water. This will keep for a week or so if refrigerated.

Hong Kong Red Bean Ice

This could really be in the dessert section—it is beautiful layered iced drink. The red beans, also known as adzuki beans, are small, dark red beans with a naturally slightly sweet flavour.

Serves 2

Ingredients

- 60 g (⅓ cup) dried adzuki beans
- 60 g (⅓ cup) coconut sugar
- 250 ml (1 cup) coconut milk
- Ice cubes
- Vanilla ice cream, to serve

Rinse the beans then soak in water overnight. Drain and transfer to a medium-sized saucepan. Add 1500 ml (6 cups) water. Bring to a boil then reduce the heat and simmer for 1 hour. Stir in the sugar and simmer for another 20 minutes.

Put ½ cup of the bean soup into a glass cup. Top up with ice cubes then pour ½ cup of coconut milk into the cup. Finally, add a scoop of vanilla ice cream on top and serve with a spoon and/or straw.

Carob Drink

In Malta, carob pods are made into a syrup known as *ġulepp* which is added to hot water or mixed with a black tea as a remedy for coughs and sore throats. A similar Egyptian recipe, known as *kharub*, is used as a refreshing cold drink. It is an interesting taste but if you find the flavour too strong on its own, it mixes well with orange juice.

Ingredients

- 200 g (1 cup) sugar
- 8 dry carob pods
- Zest and juice of 1 lemon
- 1 cinnamon stick
- 1000 ml (4 cups) water

Break the pods up into chunks or crush them with a rolling pin. Put them in a saucepan with the water and cinnamon, bring to a boil, and then turn the heat off and allow the pods to steep for a few hours. Add the sugar, lemon zest, and lemon juice. Bring it back to the boil and lower the heat, simmering it for 5 minutes. Set aside and allow to cool. Strain through muslin then either serve straight away or bottle it and store in the refrigerator for up to 2 weeks.

Tamarind Syrup

Tamarind syrup has a complex sweet-tart flavour which is very refreshing when served with sparkling water. This is the Egyptian version. In Mexico, the pulp of the pods is often retained, giving a thicker syrup flavoured with added fresh lime juice.

Ingredients

- 250 g (8 oz) dried tamarind
- 1500 ml (6 cups) water
- 400 g (2 cups) white sugar

Wash the tamarind, then boil with the water for 5 minutes and leave it to steep for 6 hours. Drain through a muslin-lined sieve. Add the sugar and boil, then pass it through a sieve again. Bottle, allow to cool. Homemade tamarind syrup will last for 2 to 3 months in the refrigerator.

Spiced Fenugreek

In Egypt, this warm and comforting drink is known as halba tea. Do not believe the numerous unsubstantiated medical claims made for fenugreek and do not overdose on it as excessive amounts can damage the liver, but the tea is an interesting drink to try on a cold day.

Serves 2

Ingredients

- 2 tbsp sesame seeds
- 2 tbsp ghee or melted butter
- 2 tsp ground fenugreek seeds
- 500 ml (2 cups) water
- 50 g (4 tbsp) sugar
- 1 tbsp toasted hazelnuts, chopped

Fry the sesame seeds and fenugreek in the ghee until golden. Add the water and sugar and cook, stirring until the mixture thickens. Pour into cups and sprinkle some chopped hazelnuts on top. Serve while warm.

BIBLIOGRAPHY

Meet the Family

Avent, Tony. "Name that Plant—The Misuse of Trademarks in Horticulture." *Plant Delights*, January 1, 2005; updated May 17, 2022. https://www.plantdelights.com/blogs/articles/name-that-plant.

Centeno-González, N.K. et al. "Late Campanian fossil of a legume fruit supports Mexico as a center of Fabaceae radiation," *Communications Biology* 4, no. 41 (January 2021): 1–8. https://doi.org/10.1038/s42003-020-01533-9.

Davidson, Alan. *The Oxford Companion to Food* (Oxford: Oxford University Press, 2014).

Herendeen, Patrick, Domingo B O S Cardoso, Fabiany Herrera, and Scott L. Wing. "Fossil papilionoids of the Bowdichia clade (Leguminosae) from the Paleogene of North America." *American Journal of Botany* 109, no. 1 (January 2022): 130–150.

Lewis, Gwilym et al. *Legumes of the World* (Royal Botanic Gardens: Kew Publishing, 2005).

Mabey, Richard. *Flora Britannica.* (London: Sinclair-Stevenson, 1996).

Wilkinson, Hazel, Patrick Herendeen, and David Dilcher. *Advances in Legume Systematics, Part 4, The Fossil Record* (Kew: Royal Botanic Gardens, 1992).

Pythagoras and the Bean

Albala, Ken. *Beans: A History* (New York: Berg Publishers, 2007).

Ambika et al. "Unraveling Origin, History, Genetics, and Strategies for Accelerated Domestication and Diversification of Food Legumes," *Frontiers in Genetics* 13 (July 2022): 1–21. https://doi.org/10.3389/fgene.2022.932430.

Cowan, C. Wesley, Patty Jo Watson, and Nancy L. Benco. *The Origins of Agriculture: An International Perspective* (Washington, DC: Smithsonian Institution Press, 1992).

Eriksson, Gunilla and Kerstin Lidén. "Dietary life histories in Stone Age Northern Europe," *Journal of Anthropological Archaeology* 32 no. 3 (September 2013): 288–302. https://doi.org/10.1016/j.jaa.2012.01.002.

Fuller, Dorian Q. and Emma L. Harvey. "The archaeobotany of Indian pulses: identification, processing and evidence for cultivation," *Environmental Archaeology* 11 no. 2 (2006): 219–246. https://doi.org/10.1179/174963106x123232.

Harris, David and Gordon Hillman eds. *Foraging and Farming: The Evolution of Plant Exploitation* (London: Routledge, 1989).

Huebbe, Patricia and Gerald Rimbach. "Historical Reflection of Food Processing and the Role of Legumes as Part of a Healthy Balanced Diet," *Foods* 9 no. 8 (August 2020): 1056. https://doi.org/10.3390/foods9081056.

Lee, Gyoung-Ah, Gary W. Crawford, Li Liu, Yuka Sasaki, and Chen Xuexiang. "Archaeological soybean (Glycine max) in East Asia: does size matter?" *PLoS One* 6 no. 11 (November 2011): 1–12. https://doi.org/10.1371/journal.pone.0026720.

Roberts, Jonathan. *Cabbages and Kings: The Origins of Fruit and Vegetables* (London: Collins, 2001).

Sonnante, Gabriella, Karl Hammer, and Domenico Pignone. "From the cradle of agriculture a handful of lentils: History of domestication," *Rendiconti Lincei* 20 (May 2009): 21–37. https://doi.org/10.1007/s12210-009-0002-7.

Treasure, Edward. R., and Mike J. Church. "Can't find a pulse? Celtic bean (*Vicia faba* L.) in British prehistory," *Environmental Archaeology* 22, no. 2 (2017), 113–127. https://doi.org/10.1080/14614103.2016.1153769.

Cultural Life

Corrado, Giandomenico. "Food history and gastronomic traditions of beans in Italy," *Journal of Ethnic Foods* 9 no. 6 (December 2022): 1–9. https://doi.org/10.1186/s42779-022-00122-x.

Flint-Hamilton, Kimberly B. "Legumes in Ancient Greece and Rome: Food, Medicine, or Poison?" *Hesperia: The Journal of the American*

School of Classical Studies at Athens 68 no. 3 (July–September 1999): 371–385. https://www.jstor.org/stable/148493.
Hastorf, Christine A. *The Social Archaeology of Food: Thinking about Eating from Prehistory to the Present* (New York: Cambridge University Press, 2017).
Hurlock, Kathryn. "The Pilgrim and the Peas and Pilgrimage by Rail: Defining acceptable pilgrimage practices in Nineteenth-Century Britain," *Cultural and Social History* 20 no. 4 (June 2023): 537–550. https://doi.org/10.1080/14780038.2023.2219493.
Myers, James R., Alice K. Formiga, and Jules Janick. "Iconography of Beans and Related Legumes Following the Columbian Exchange," *Frontiers in Plant Science* 13 (March 2022): 1–20. https://doi.org/10.3389/fpls.2022.851029.
Tatar, Maria ed. *The Classic Fairy Tales: Texts, Criticism* (New York: W.W. Norton, 1999).

Cultivation and Processing

Bird, Richard. *Growing Shoots, Peas and Beans: A Directory of Varieties and How to Cultivate Them Successfully* (London: Lorenz Books, 2015).
Birmingham Food Revolution Initiative. *Full of Beans Kids' Club Growing Guide* (Birmingham City Council, 2024). https://www.birmingham.gov.uk/download/downloads/id/29963/fob_growing_guide_kids_club_2024.pdf.
Chamberlain, Lucy. *RHS Grow Food Anywhere: How to Plant the Right Crops in the Right Place and Help Your Garden Thrive* (London: Dorling Kindersley, 2025).
Dove, Helana. *The Kew Gardener's Guide to Growing Vegetables: The Art and Science to Grow Your Own Vegetables* (London: White Lion Publishing, 2020).
Jason, Dan, Hilary Malone, and Alison Malone Eathorne. *The Power of Pulses: Saving the World with Peas, Beans, Chickpeas, Favas and Lentils* (Madeira Park, British Columbia: Douglas and McIntyre, 2016).
Li Liu et al. "Fermented beverage and food storage in 13,000 y-old stone mortars at Raqefet Cave, Israel: Investigating Natufian ritual feasting," *Journal of Archaeological Science: Reports* 21 (October 2018): 783–793. https://doi.org/10.1016/j.jasrep.2018.08.008.
Stocks, Christopher. *Forgotten Fruits: The stories behind Britain's traditional fruit and vegetables* (London: Windmill, 2008).

Young, Susan. *Growing Beans: A Diet for Healthy People & Planet* (East Meon, Hampshire, UK: Permanent Publications, 2022).

Pulses and Health

Adamcová, Anežka, Kristian Holtz Laursen, and Nicolai Zederkopff Ballin. "Lectin Activity in Commonly Consumed Plant-Based Foods: Calling for Method Harmonization and Risk Assessment," *Foods* 10 no. 11 (November 2021): 2796. https://doi.org/10.3390/foods10112796.

Ahmed, Salah Noori. "Do favic patients resume fava beans ingestion later in their life, a study for this, and a new hypothesis for favism etiology," *Hematology/Oncology and Stem Cell Therapy* 6 no. 1 (March 2013): 9–13. https://doi.org/10.1016/j.hemonc.2013.03.002.

Belsey, Mark A. "The epidemiology of favism," *Bull World Health Organ* 48, no. 1 (1973): 1–13. PMID: 4541143; PMCID: PMC2481045.

Beretta, Alice, Matteo Manuelli, and Hellas Cena. "Favism: Clinical Features at Different Ages," *Nutrients* 15, no. 2 (January 2023): 343. https://doi.org/10.3390/nu15020343.

Blackwell, Elizabeth. *A Curious Herbal* (London: 1737–1739).

Du Toit, George et al. "Randomized Trial of Peanut Consumption in Infants at Risk for Peanut Allergy," *New England Journal of Medicine* 372 no. 9 (July 2016): 803–13. https://doi.org/10.1056/nejmx150044.

Leyva, Rodolfo, Miguel Da Silva Ramos, and Joseph Sakshaug. "Breaking Bread: Investigating the Role of Ethnic Food in Potentiating Outgroup Tolerance," *Sage Open* 15 no. 3 (July 2025). https://doi.org/10.1177/21582440251378940.

Loke, Atul et al. *Pulses: nutritious seeds for a sustainable future* (Rome: The Food and Agriculture Organization of the United Nations, 2016).

Mastrorilli, Carla et al. "IgE-Mediated Legume Allergy: A Pediatric Perspective," *Journal of Personalized Medicine* 14 no. 9 (August 2024): 898. https://doi.org/10.3390/jpm14090898.

Mullins, Amy P. and Bahram H. Arjmandi. "Health Benefits of Plant-Based Nutrition: Focus on Beans in Cardiometabolic Diseases," *Nutrients* 13 no. 2 (February 2021): 519. https://doi.org/10.3390/nu13020519.

Pollan, Michael. *In Defense of Food: An Eater's Manifesto* (New York: Penguin, 2008).

Rijntjes, Michel. "Knowing Your Beans in Parkinson's Disease: A Critical Assessment of Current Knowledge about Different Beans and Their Compounds in the Treatment of Parkinson's Disease and in Animal

Models," *Parkinson's Disease* (October 2019): 1–9. https://doi.org/10.1155/2019/1349509.

Recipes

Eden, Caroline. *Black Sea: Dispatches and Recipes—Through Darkness and Light* (London: Quadrille, 2018).

Good Housekeeping Institute. *Good Housekeeping Cookery Book* rev. ed. (London: Ebury Press, 1985).

Gregory, Patricia R. *Bean Banquets from Boston to Bombay* (Santa Barbara, California: Woodbridge Press, 1992).

Jason, Dan, Hilary Malone, and Alison Malone Eathorne. *The Power of Pulses: Saving the World with Peas, Beans, Chickpeas, Favas and Lentils* (Madeira Park, British Columbia: Douglas and McIntyre, 2016).

Maidment, Eleanor. *Pulse: Modern Recipes with Beans, Peas & Lentils* (London: Ryland, Peters & Small, 2025).

Mehdawy, Magda. *My Egyptian Grandmother's Kitchen: Traditional Dishes Sweet and Savoury* (Cairo: American University in Cairo Press, 2006).

Lawson, Nigella. *How to Eat: The Pleasures and Principles of Good Food* (London: Chatto and Windus, 1998).

Ottolenghi, Yotam and Sami Tamimi. *Ottolenghi: The Cookbook* (London: Ebury Press, 2008).

The Book of Sent Soví: Medieval Recipes from Catalonia. Edited by Joan Santanach. Translated by Robin Vogelzang. Suffolk: Barcino-Tamesis, 2008.

Sodha, Meera. *Dinner: 120 vegan and vegetarian recipes for the most important meal of the day* (London: Fig Tree, 2024).

WEBSITES AND ASSOCIATIONS

Allergy UK is a British medical charity dedicated to supporting those with allergies. www.allergyuk.org.

Beans and Herbs have a bean club allowing access to many unusual and heirloom cultivars of beans. www.beansandherbs.co.uk.

The Bean Institute is a useful source of information on nutrition and recipes. https://beaninstitute.com.

California-based Blue House Farm supply heirloom beans grown in San Gregorio. https://bluehousefarm.com.

Garden Organic, for advice on growing without chemicals. www.gardenorganic.org.uk.

Hodmedod's is a UK supplier of pulses. Their website includes many useful recipes. https://hodmedods.co.uk.

Rancho Gordo supplies a wide range of heirloom beans in the United States. https://www.ranchogordo.com.

The National Vegetable Society provides guides to growing vegetables for exhibition. www.nvsuk.org.uk.

The Royal Horticultural Society, the UK's leading gardening charity, has many online growing guides including beans for drying, broad beans, peas, runner beans and soya beans. www.rhs.org.uk.

Plants of the World Online, the database of the Royal Botanic Gardens, Kew. www.kew.org.

ACKNOWLEDGEMENTS

My thanks go to all the members of the dietetic team at the Norfolk and Norwich University Hospital for freely sharing their knowledge, food expertise, cooking skills, and good humour over many years. I would like to express particular appreciation to the allergy team, Dr. Sara Abdelgalil, Dr. Alex Brightwell, Dr. Satish Chandran, Liz Ingham, Iona Mullan, Maria Birchall, Charlotte Tompkins, Ann Thompson, Sam Courteney, and Beverley Burkill. Thank you to those colleagues, friends and family members who have suggested their 'must include' for the recipe section. Avery Robinson at Equinox has edited with great patience and thoroughness. And a special thank you to Ash and Jonathan Harland who have unflinchingly eaten my somewhat erratic cookery all their lives.

INDEX OF NAMES AND SUBJECTS

Page numbers in *italics* refer to the illustrations.

INDEX OF RECIPES

www.ingramcontent.com/pod-product-compliance
Lightning Source LLC
LaVergne TN
LVHW010945271026
851073LV00023B/255
9781800508774